# All M

## Why She Spoke – Why She Wept at La Salette

By Fr. Marcel Schlewer, M.S.
Translated by Fr. James P. O'Reilly, M.S.

Missionaries of La Salette Corporation
915 Maple Avenue
Hartford, CT 06114-2330, USA
website: www.lasalette.org

**First edition (French):** *Choisissez Donc La Vie: Une lecture du message de Notre-Dame de La Salette*, 1996

**First Edition (English):** *All My People; Why she spoke – Why she wept at La Salette*, September 19, 1998

**Second (and expanded) edition:** This expanded edition contains a wider selection of visuals. Copyright @ February 2, 2019 by Missionaries of Our Lady of La Salette, Province of Mary, Mother of the Americas, 915 Maple Avenue, Hartford, CT, 06106-2330, USA

**Imprimi Potest:** Rev. Fr. Rene J. Butler, M.S., Provincial Superior Missionaries of Our Lady of La Salette, Province of Mary, Mother of the Americas, 915 Maple Avenue Hartford, CT 06106-2330, USA

Printed in the United States of America

Editor: Fr. Ron Gagné, M.S.

Booklet Design and Digital Formatting: Jack Battersby and Fr. Ron Gagné, M.S.

This and other La Salette titles are available in paper, e-book and audiobook formats at: www.Amazon.com, itunes.Apple.com, and www.lasalette.org

ISBN: 978-1-946956-26-2

"I call heaven and earth today to witness against you: I have set before you life and death, the blessing and the curse. *Choose life, then,* that you and your descendants may live,20by loving the Lord, your God, obeying his voice, and holding fast to him" (Deuteronomy 30: 19-20a).

To:

AHCENE, summarily executed in 1961 at the age 17, in Little Kabylia;

And

IQBAL MASIH, a Pakistani child slave and a Christian, who denounced the massive exploitation of children in carpet factories. He was murdered on Easter Sunday, April 16, 1995 at 19 years of age.

# Contents

# Preface

Marcel Schlewer, a member of the religious congregation of the Missionaries of Our Lady of La Salette, invites us to reflect anew on the message of La Salette in the light of the Scriptures and, in particular, of the admonition of Deuteronomy: "Choose life, then!" These essays are presented to us in language that is strong, courageous, and at times even daring.

Fr. Marcel Schlewer, M.S., author of this book

This book testifies to a basic conviction: "Beloved, you (are) aliens and sojourners" (1 Peter 2:11a). The human condition is that of a pilgrim, with no lasting place here on earth, always a stranger, yet impelled to move, to go forward, aspiring to "a better homeland, a heavenly one" (Hebrews 11:16).

Here we see the paradox of Christian life which Mary recalls at La Salette: My Son is with the Father, and the Father is always in your midst; he is present at the very core of your lives. Our Blessed Mother brings this out wonderfully when, speaking of the spoiled wheat, she says to Maximin: *"But you, my child. you must surely have seen some once when you were near the farm of Coin with your father."*

We await the world to come, "the heavenly Jerusalem", where complete harmony will prevail. But this expectation would be an illusion, an evasion, if we were not anxious to assist our brothers and sisters in building a better world here below, and to do all in our power to make this world more harmonious, more just, more fraternal. Jesus stated that "one does not live by bread alone" (Matthew 4:4a) and that anyone who lives without love is sick, out of joint and close to death (see Matthew 5:43-45).

This book takes a hard look at a paradox: Christians willingly preach

i

to others about love of neighbor, while at the same time tolerating inhuman and unjust social structures in which it is impossible to live as brothers and sisters.

True, the building of a more fraternal world is not identical with the definitive realization of the Kingdom of God. Nevertheless, we would betray the demands of the Gospel if we spoke to men and women about eternal salvation while failing to do everything we can to give their lives on this earth a more human countenance.

The message of La Salette reminds us of salvation history, and the author invites us to revisit it so as to discover two things:

> - The ever-present temptation to move in every direction, experimenting with what is good and what is evil, but with no effort at discernment;

> - The Choice of Life. This life is none other than God, offered to us as "the way, the truth and the life" (John 14:6a; 8:12) and who hopes for a generous response from us. "The Lord is my shepherd ... He guides me along right paths" (Psalm 23:1b,3).

To place our footsteps in those of Christ and to follow him is the only possible response. "So be imitators of God, as beloved children, and live in love, as Christ loved us and handed himself over for us" (Ephesians 5:1-2a). Such was the intensely loving exhortation of St. Paul to the first Christians.

That is the challenge which is now proposed to us. May we savor and appreciate the opportunity to live it out!

*Isidro Augusto Perin, M.S.*
Superior General of the Missionaries of Our Lady of La Salette
Rome, Christmas 1995.

Fr. Isidro Perrin, M.S., fifteenth
La Salette Superior General

# Letter of
# Cardinal Carlo Maria Martini

Archbishop of Milan

Reverend Father Marcel Schlewer,

I am happy to learn of the imminent publication of a new book on the meaning of the message of Our Lady of La Salette, because I myself, during a pilgrimage to this shrine, pondered that very subject.

What is the import of the fact that the Blessed Virgin weeps? What reality underlies the image of Mary's shedding tears for us today?

Cardinal Carlo Maria
Martini, S.J. (1927-2012);
Wiki-commons

I found the answer in these words of Jacques Maritain:

> "If the Virgin wept, if she spoke thus, it means that, of all the signs which are accessible to the human mind and heart, no other could better express the ineffable reality of what takes place in heaven. Language which presupposes the incompatibility of sorrow and blessedness, sins more by defect than by excess. The tears of the Queen of heaven are still far from revealing to us the supreme horror which God and his Mother feel toward sin, and the infinite mercy they feel toward sinners."

Consequently, Our Lady wishes to make known to us that we lack a sense of that sinfulness which is the cause of her tears. We must therefore suppose in God a kind of suffering, due to our present situation and in particular that of Christians, both individually and as communities. God is really affected by our situation: infidelities, sins, insults, violence, war and dishonesty. Feeling keenly our offenses, God is incensed at the harm humans inflict on each other, while rejoicing to see all the good we do on behalf of the "least ones". God is saddened on witnessing whatever is opposed to the divine plan of love.

Hence, we are invited to understand the intimate meaning of God's love for all, a love which Mary pours into our hearts as a grace. And I am certain that your book will be a precious help to all in coming to a deeper understanding of this mystery.

With my most cordial greetings in the Lord,

Yours,
*Carlo Maria C. Martini, S.J.*
Milan, October 30, 1995

# Foreword

To write on the theology of La Salette, on the spiritual meaning of the message, is what I have been asked to do. As I put the finishing touches on this work begun over thirty years ago, I recall many faces, friendly or indifferent, rarely hostile, who would look at you inquiringly, even skeptically, as if to ask: "La Salette? How is this relevant today? That archaic, threatening discourse has nothing to do with the Gospel." I am reminded of the scoffing remark made by Nathanael. To Philip, who invited him to come and meet the Messiah, the Liberator, he replied: "Can anything good come from Nazareth?"

"Can anything good come from La Salette?" But perhaps the reader remembers Philip's answer: "Come and see!" For there is much at stake in the message of La Salette, despite some seemingly disconcerting elements. To bring this out more fully, I will cite the cry of two men who are also priests, Father Georges Zabelka and the Abbé Pierre.

Father Zabelka was a military chaplain at the air base from which the bombers took off for Hiroshima and Nagasaki. Many years later he wrote: "Like most chaplains I spoke out clearly and firmly on certain subjects, such as killing or torturing prisoners. But there were certain areas where things were not said so clearly. The destruction of civilian populations has always been condemned by the Church, and if a soldier had come to me to ask if he could shoot a child in the head, I would have told him firmly no.

Fr. George Benedict Zabelka (1915-1992), a Catholic U.S. Army Air Force chaplain

"But in 1945 the island of Tinian was the largest air base in the world. Three planes could take off every minute. Many of these planes flew towards Japan for the precise purpose, not of killing a child or a civilian, but of massacring hundreds, thousands and tens of thousands of civilians and children. And I said nothing. Yes, I knew that civilians were being killed, and I knew it at a time when perhaps others did not know it. And yet I never preached even one sermon against this murder of civilians in the presence of those who were committing it ... As far as I know, no American cardinal and no bishop condemned these massive air raids ..." Such an avowal is horrific; "tens of thousands of people were killed ... and I said nothing ... No bishop expressed opposition to these massive air raids."

I think of this priest as I reread Mary's message. She came to reveal to her people the mortal danger into which they had strayed and in which they had become entangled. She came to say to her people with all the authority of her tears that if they do not choose the **One who is life itself**, her Son, then they are moving towards a great famine, both material and especially spiritual, and towards the death of little children. The statistics from UNICEF are

vi

terrifying: from 30,000 to 40,000 children die each day.

And then there is another cry, that of the Abbé Pierre. He is well known as the voice of the excluded and the "voiceless". Less well-known is his passion for speaking about God to the people of today. Let us listen to him: "We must avenge both God and humanity. God has been insulted by being presented (often by our catechism and theology) as the all-powerful dominator. We must avenge this insult by showing God as the all-powerful captive of love. We must also avenge humanity for being horribly deceived as regards the meaning of freedom. True, freedom is the highest value existing in the world, but men and women have been deceived into seeing freedom as an end in itself. How then can we be surprised that young people take drugs or give in to despair to the point of suicide, for they are disgusted with everything in life.

"Freedom, yes, but for what? What does freedom mean to these young people, if no one shows them the truth? And that is where humanity must be avenged. Men and women are free so as to be able, in their turn, to love; liberty is the means which makes a person more than a thing; it is the means enabling us to be like God, who becomes, even at the cost of suffering, a willing prisoner of the suffering of others."

In the same way the Virgin of La Salette comes to speak to us about God and humanity without ever separating them from each other, and invites us, in the midst of all our problems, economic, political, and social (the potatoes and the wheat), to live, in union with Christ, in loving submission to God's plan for the human race. Mary thus seeks to avenge both God and humanity.

Paul Claudel (1868-1955), a devout French Catholic, a poet, dramatist and diplomat; photo: United States Library of Congress

So, having evoked the faces of skeptics and questioners, I must also confess to being the amazed and admiring witness of many men and women who were deeply influenced by Mary's tears! Very often life had wounded them profoundly, and they let themselves be grasped. As the great Paul Claudel said: "What a strained theology finds hard to justify, the heart sees at once."

*La Salette, August 6, 1995*

# Accepting and Understanding the Message

Three phases of the La Salette Apparition

Church history, from the 19th century on, mentions several Marian apparitions:

- 1830, at the rue du Bae in Paris, Our Lady appeared to Catherine Laboure and gave her the Miraculous Medal.

- 1846, at La Salette, in the French Alps.

- 1858, at Lourdes, between February 11 and July 16, Mary came sixteen times to ask Bernadette Soubirous to tell people to pray and do penance.

- 1870-1871, at Pontmain, Mary appeared in the department of Mayenne to ask people to pray for peace ..

- 1917, at Fatima, in Portugal, three children heard her call to prayer and conversion.

- 1932, at Beauraing, in Belgium, she appeared to five children between a street and a railroad track and renewed her appeal for prayer and conversion.

The following year, at Banneux, she called herself "The Virgin of the Poor" and spoke to three children.

## Why Apparitions?

The Church, in its great prudence, declared these apparitions authentic only after long and meticulous inquiries. One could ask, why do Marian apparitions occur in the first place? Do we need them? Did we not receive the fullness of revelation when the Son of God appeared here on earth in our midst, taking on our human nature?

Nevertheless, the Church throughout its history has recognized a certain number of apparitions. It does so only to the extent that they lead us back to the one great apparition, that of Jesus Christ who came to reveal to us the face of God. So much so that we should have more of an appetite for the Gospel, the Word of God, than for apparitions! Mary's message at La Salette is a reminder of this Word of God.

## Two Poor Children

To whom did the Virgin choose to appear? Generally, to the poor. At La Salette she appeared to two children, Maximin Giraud and Melanie Calvat. Maximin was a boy of eleven years of age. His father, Monsieur Giraud, a wheelwright, lived in Corps and repaired the wheels of stage-coaches. He was a man who felt no need of God and had not set foot inside a church for twenty years. His first wife, who was Maximin's mother, died. He remarried; but it was hard to make ends meet, and Maximin was left to himself. Since in those days attendance at school was not obligatory, he skipped both school and catechism. He spent most of his time roaming the streets while watching over his goat. But he was careless. One day he even let the goat strangle itself. So, when on September 14 Pierre Selme, a peasant at Les Ablandins, one of the thirteen hamlets of the commune of La Salette, came to ask Mr. Giraud to loan him his son for one week, Giraud was very hesitant. But he finally let himself be persuaded and Maximin left for Les Ablandins in the company of Pierre Selme.

It was there that, for the first time, on September 17, Maximin would see Melanie Calvat. Born in 1831, she too was a native of Corps. Her father, Monsieur Mathieu, known also as Calvat, was a woodcutter and made planks from trees. But unemployment was high; most of the time he took odd jobs to feed his seven children, with little success. So it was that Melanie, the eldest, was hired out as shepherdess in hamlets around Corps: Sainte-Luce, Quet-en-Beaumont, etc., and during this month of September 1846-with the Pra family at Les Ablandins. She attended neither school nor catechism and had not been admitted to First Communion.

The two children, therefore, did not know each other when their paths crossed at Les Ablandins on September 17. On the 18th, they watched over their respective herds on the mountain, at some distance from each other. Melanie was reserved and uncommunicative, whereas Maximin was much more expansive and ·eager to make acquaintances. And once they realized they were both from Corps, it was settled: they would ascend the mountain together the next day, September 19, 1846.

Nothing unusual occurred that morning. At noon, as was customary, they led their cows to drink at what was called "the animals' spring", where a kind of dam retained the water flowing from higher up; that is now the area under the bridge to the Holy Mountain's shrine buildings. Then they led the cows to a relatively level grassy area to rest; this area is today the winding path used for processions. The children themselves climbed a little higher, where the cistern is now, to the "people's spring", an abundant natural spring now serving the needs of the pilgrims' hostel. After eating their lunch, they went back down to the "little spring", a spring which was usually dry, like so many mountain springs that flow only during the spring thaw or after the heavy autumn rains. On September 21, or just two days after the apparition, it was observed that the spring had begun to flow anew, and it has never ceased flowing since.

At this spot, then, the two children allowed themselves a little siesta, about half an hour. Melanie was the first to awake; she shook her companion. "Mémin, quick! Come and look for our cows!" From the bottom of a gully, one's view is very limited. So Melanie climbed the slope to the southeast. At the top she turned around and was relieved to find the cows resting peacefully where they had left them.

She started to go back down to fetch the basket of provisions she had left on a sort of stone bench. Halfway down, she stopped, glued to the spot, and cried out, " Mémin, quick! Come and look at this great light!" At the very spot where they had slept, they saw a globe of fire, "as if the sun had fallen there." They were frightened but Maximin was the first to regain his composure. "Melanie," he said, "keep your stick and I will keep mine and if it does anything to us, I'll give it a good whack!"

## A Woman in Tears

They stood there, looking intently as the globe of fire swirled and gradually grew in size. A moment later they perceived within it a woman seated, in tears. Maximin would later say, "I thought it was a mother from Valjoufrey who had been beaten by her children and who had fled to the mountain to cry her heart out." He would have liked to say to her, "Oh, don't cry, we're going to help you."

4

Ordinarily the Virgin Mary is not represented to us in this manner. It is good for us to pause, to look at her for a minute and to ask ourselves the question children often ask: "Why is she crying?" We can also point out a coincidence of which the two shepherds were unaware. In the liturgy of that period, the third Sunday of September was the feast of Our Lady of Seven Sorrows, now celebrated on September 15. So, at the very hour when the apparition was taking place, on that Saturday, September 19, 1846, the Church was singing, at the first Vespers of this feast, "See with what an abundance of tears is bathed the face of the Virgin Mother. o all you that pass by the way, attend and see if there be any sorrow like to my sorrow!" The children, of course, knew nothing of this.

Early German holy card of the children discovering Our Weeping Mother, seated on a stone

## Do Not Be Afraid

They just kept looking. A few moments later, the Beautiful Lady, as they spontaneously called her without knowing her identity, stood up and spoke her first words: *"Come near, my children, do not be afraid. I am here to tell you great news."* They did not understand these words spoken in French, for in that region only the local dialect was spoken in those days. Nevertheless, her voice was so gentle and maternal that their fear disappeared entirely. "It was like music," they said later. Now they hurried down to meet their visitor, while she took a few steps in their direction. The two children huddled so close to her that, as Maximin later observed, "No one could have slipped in between her and us." They listened to her and gazed at her intently.

Afterwards, when they tried to describe her, they depicted her as tall and majestic. She was dressed like the local peasant women, namely, wearing a long dress, an apron, a shawl around her shoulders, and a bonnet on her head. Some features of her costume were unique: garlands of multicolored roses adorned her shoulders, her waist, her shoes and her head, forming a crown beneath a diadem of light. Thus, Mary appeared at La Salette as a servant in servant's garb, but as a queen as well. Around her shoulders she also wore a heavy chain which seemed to crush and weigh her down-the symbol of the misery and sin of her people. Mary appears here as enchained by whatever imprisons her children.

Around her neck was another, much smaller chain, from which a crucifix was suspended on her breast. The crucifix was some eight to ten inches long, dazzlingly bright, the most luminous portion of the globe of fire. The light embraced both the Blessed Virgin and the children, and they noticed they did not cast any shadow. The arms of the crucifix bore the instruments of the Passion: a hammer and pincers, as if Our Lady were coming to say to us: "I resolved to know nothing while I was with you except Jesus Christ, and him crucified" (1 Cor. 2:2), and to invite us to choose between the hammer, symbol of the sin that crucifies Christ's Body today, and the pincers symbolizing conversion and liberation. This crucifix sums up the La Salette message rather effectively. But what exactly did Mary say to the children?

## Mary's Message

*If my people will not submit, I shall be forced to let fall the arm of my son. It is so strong, so heavy, that I can no longer withhold it. For how long a time do I suffer for you! If I would not have my Son abandon you, I am compelled to pray to him without ceasing; and as for you, you take no heed of it! However much you pray, however much you do, you will never recompense the pains I have taken for you.*

*Six days have I given you to labor; the seventh I have kept for myself; and no one will give it to me. It is this which makes the arm of my Son so heavy. Those who drive the carts cannot swear without introducing the name of my Son. These are the two things which make the arm of my Son so heavy.*

*If the harvest is spoiled, it is all on your account. I gave you warning last*

*year with the potato harvest, but you did not heed it.
On the contrary, when you found them spoiled,
you swore, you took the name of my Son in
vain. They will continue to spoil, so that by
Christmas there will be none left.*

Not understanding the French expression,
*pommes de terre (potatoes),* Melanie looked
inquiringly at Maximin. But the Beautiful
Lady anticipated her question. *"Ah! my
children, you do not understand. Well, wait,
I will say it otherwise."*

And she repeated in their dialect what
she had just said about the ruined harvest,
before going on: *"If you have wheat, it is no
good to sow it; all that you sow the insects
will eat, and what comes up will fall into
dust when you thresh it.*

Early German holy card of
Mary standing, speaking with
the two children

*"There will come a great famine. Before the famine comes, the little children
under seven years of age will be seized with trembling and will die in the
arms of the persons holding them; the rest will do penance by the famine.
The walnuts will become bad, the grapes will rot."*

At this point in the message, Maximin could see the Lady's lips move
but could hear nothing. The same thing happened to Melanie a few
moments later. After the Blessed Virgin had disappeared, the children discussed this in a delightful exchange:

"What was she saying when she was saying nothing?" asked Melanie.

"Oh, she told me something, but it's just for me and I won't tell you
anything."

"Oh, good, I'm glad, because she told me something too, just for me,
and I won't tell you either."

Thus, the children discovered they had each received a secret, in
French. They would never care to discuss it.

But in 1851, the Metropolitan Archbishop of Lyons succeeded in persuading the Bishop of Grenoble to have the two witnesses put their secrets in writing—something they were at first most reluctant to do. These secrets were sent to Pope Pius IX, but they were never published either by him or by his successors. When, some years later, Father Giraud, the second Superior General of the Missionaries of Our Lady of La Salette, asked the Pope about the secrets in the course of an audience, the Pope replied: "Well, if you do not repent, you will all perish ...," —words from the Gospel of Luke (13:5).

The Virgin then resumed her message in the children's dialect:

*"If they are converted, the stones and rocks will become mounds of wheat, and the potatoes will be self-sown in the fields.*

*"Do you say your prayers well, my children?* "Oh, not very well, Madame," they answered.

*"Ah! my children, you must be sure to say them well, evening and morning, even if you say only an Our Father and a Hail Mary; but when you have time and can do better, you should say more.*

*"In the summer none go to Mass but a few somewhat aged women. The rest work on Sunday all summer long; and in winter, when they do not know what to do, they go to Mass only to mock at religion. During Lent, they go to the meat market like dogs. Have you never seen wheat that is spoiled, my children?"*

"Oh, no, Madame."

*"But you, my child"*, she insisted, addressing Maximin, *"you must surely have seen some, near the farm of Coin. The owner of the field told your father, 'Come and see how my wheat is spoiling.' The two of you went over together. Your father took two or three ears of wheat into his hand, and rubbed them, and everything crumbled into dust. Then when you were returning home and were only half an hour's distance from Corps, your father gave you a piece of bread and said to you: 'Here, my child, eat some bread still this year; I don't know who will eat any next year, if the wheat goes on like that!'"*

Maximin replied: "That's right, Madame; just at this moment I didn't remember."

Then the Lady added, in French:

*"Well, my children, you will make this known to all my people."*

She then stepped around the children, crossing the brook flowing from the "people's spring". Without turning around, she repeated her final injunction, this time with greater emphasis: *"Very well, my children, be sure to make this known to all my people."* These were her last words.

As she climbed the slope, the children followed. When she reached the top, she stood motionless about five feet above the ground, looked up to heaven and

Early German holy card of Mary disappearing into light

then looked one last time at the children, who by now stood in front of her. Then she gradually disappeared into the light, as Maximin vainly reached for one of the multicolored roses on her feet. "She melted like butter in a frying pan," he would later say in his colorful way.

Melanie said to her companion: "Perhaps it was a great saint!"

"If we had known," said Maximin, "we would have asked her to take us with her."

## The First Account of the Apparition

This comment of the children is interesting; it shows they did not know who had spoken to them. The first person to guess her identity was "Mère Caron" an old woman who lived at Les Ablandins and to whom Maximin called out upon returning from the mountain that evening. "Hey, Mère Caron, did you see a Beautiful Lady on fire above the valley? She spoke with Melanie and me this afternoon on the mountain." The old lady listened dumb founded, incredulous. But Maximin insisted "If you don't believe me, then call Melanie!" The girl was already busy at her chores in the stable. They went to get her, and thus in the farmhouse kitchen at Les Ablandins, she gave her first account of the apparition. And the old woman concluded: "It is the Virgin that these children have seen, for there is only one in Heaven whose Son governs, and that is the Blessed Virgin." Then she turned reproachfully to her son-in-law. "After this, go now and work again on Sundays!"

The next day was in fact a Sunday. It was decided that the children should go to the parish priest, to acquaint him with the facts, before Mass. He in turn, weeping and stammering, spoke of the event to his congregation. Immediately after Mass the mayor of La Salette, at a regular meeting of his municipal council, expressed concern over the pastor's loss of composure and observed that people were starting to talk about the two children.

That afternoon the mayor, to find out the truth, went to Les Ablandins to interrogate the children. To his great surprise, only Melanie was present. Maximin had already been brought back to his father that morning by Pierre Selme after the meeting with the parish priest. It is important to note that the children only became acquainted with each other on the eve of the Apparition and were separated from each other the day following it. So, the mayor interviewed Melanie, and hoped to obtain her silence. He tried to bribe her with a gold coin; then he resorted to threats. Melanie had only one response, "I have been told to tell it, and tell it I will." The mayor admitted defeat. After his departure, however, three peasants who were present, Messieurs Pra, Selme and Moussier, had a brilliant idea: why not write down the Beautiful Lady's discourse at Melanie's dictation, in French and in dialect. As a result, we have a solid document which dates from the day after the morrow of the Apparition and is known as the Pra Account.

Now let us briefly review a few historical landmarks. On October 6, 1846, Philibert de Bruillard, the bishop of Grenoble, published an admonition addressed to the priests of the diocese, asking them not to discuss the event. This was a prudent measure, but he lost no time in gathering all the pertinent information. He learned, for example, that ten days after the apparition, about a thousand people were counted on the mountain. The following winter, which was unusually severe, the crowds continued to come in steadily increasing numbers.

## The Church's Inquiry

For the first anniversary of the Apparition, crowd estimates range between 40,000 and 100,000 pilgrims. The bishop, who was regularly kept informed by the priests stationed at La Salette and Corps, now appointed two fact-finding commissions to gather documentation and testimonies. Afterward, another commission, some of whose members were known opponents, met several times before presenting its conclusion in November of 1847, to wit: "The children were neither deceived nor deceivers." By this time the bishop was personally convinced, but, as a matter of prudence, he continued over a four-year period to seek the advice of a number of bishops, cardinals and the Pope himself.

The Abbé Lagier speaking with the two children about the Apparition

A number of accounts of the event exist, some of them more or less fanciful. Let us note only the most historically accurate. In 1846 the Laurent account was written by people from Corps who knew the local dialect. In the spring of 1847, Fr. Lagier, a priest and native of Corps, pastor of Saint-Pierre-de-Cherennes in the lower Isere valley, came to visit his ailing father and thought he could unmask the children's story as a hoax. He interrogated them at great length, carefully wrote down their every response, and left convinced of the truth of the Apparition. This document, therefore, is to be taken seriously.

Meanwhile the civil authorities were becoming concerned also. Following instructions from the Ministry of Cult, Master Long, the notary and mayor of Corps, began another inquiry, and his report, written in French and in the local dialect, is also a reliable record. This matter of documentation may be profitably pursued in the three volumes published by Father Jean Stern, a Missionary of Our Lady of La Salette, and containing all the documentary evidence on La Salette up to November 4, 1854.

## The Pastoral Letter of Bishop Philibert de Bruillard

On September 19, 1851, Bishop de Bruillard published a pastoral letter in which he recognized the authenticity of the Apparition. Here is the essential passage:

"We judge that the Apparition of the Blessed Virgin to two cowherds on the 19th of September 1846, on a mountain of the Alpine chain, situated in the parish of La Salette, in the archpresbytery of Corps, bears within itself all the characteristics of truth, and that the faithful have grounds for believing it indubitable and certain."

There was therefore both discernment and approval by the Church. Nevertheless, no one is required to believe in the Apparition. Still, why should we not be attentive to this gift of God offered to us through the manifestation of the Blessed Virgin at La Salette?

## Understanding the Message

Bp. Philibert de Bruillard (1765-1860), founder of the La Salette Missionaries

After this brief account of the events, it is important to return to the question of Mary's intention. Why did she come to this remote corner of the Alps? What did she wish to communicate to the people of that period and to us today? This is not an easy message to understand and, when one first encounters it, it is disconcerting. But, after all, what is surprising about that? Whenever God intervenes in our lives, upheaval follows. Let us then try to accept Mary's message, but without giving up the effort to understand it, without separating faith and understanding!

*There are three ways of reading the La Salette message:*

- The Blessed Virgin is a good preacher. She speaks the language of those whom she is immediately addressing: the dialect. She speaks about the hard life of the local peasantry. And they easily understood the message, because she knew how to speak of God by speaking about their everyday lives. But this does not mean her message is meant only for them. On the contrary, she wishes to address "all her people." When Melanie was asked what "all her people" meant, she replied, "Everybody, of course."

- The Blessed Virgin speaks in her mother tongue, as it were, in biblical categories. The message is woven together from the words and expressions of Sacred Scripture, particularly as found in the prophets.

- In the Bible, the prophet's mission is not, first and foremost, to predict the future, still less to announce calamities. First of all, he speaks in the name of and in the place of God. And so, when Mary in her discourse says: *"I have given you six days to labor,"* it is not she who gave them to us, but evidently God. Anyone who knows Scripture is aware that the prophets speak this way, in the first person. They are the spokespersons of none other than God!

# Now Let Us Consider the Message in Detail

*"Come near, my children, do not be afraid."* The expression *"Do not be afraid"* is basic. It was the invitation of Jesus after he had risen from the dead and appeared to his disciples, and the first words of John Paul II as pope. Do not be afraid, believers, to present yourselves as such to the world. We must not be afraid of God or fear God's intervention in our lives, but accept being unsettled, being disturbed.

*"I am here to tell you great news …"*, the great news of the Gospel, that same good news which the shepherds heard on Christmas night: "Do not be afraid; for behold, I proclaim to you good news" (Luke 2:10a).

*"If my people will not submit ..."*: here we have two expressions which typify the profoundly biblical meaning of Mary's message. Already, a hundred years before the Second Vatican Council, she speaks of "the People of God." She comes to draw us away from our religious individualism ("One soul alone have I to save") to situate us in the midst of this people and remind us that we also are responsible members of that people.

*"To submit"*: who likes to submit? If Mary uses this term, it is not to lecture us, but to remind us of something essential which is at the heart of the New Testament. In our human world all things find their meaning in Jesus Christ, God in human flesh. One could cite numerous Scripture texts to support this assertion. Let us take Paul's first letter to the Corinthians: "When everything is subjected to him, then the Son himself will [also] be subjected to the one who subjected everything to him, so that God may be all in all" (1 Corinthians 15:28).

Here one finds the verb "to subject" used three times in one verse! This basic truth is taken up again in the Council decree entitled, *"Pastoral Constitution on the Church in the Modern World."* At the end of each chapter we find the same thought expressed: The Word of God, who became flesh, comes to give meaning to human realities (*Gaudium et spes*, 10, 22, 38, 45). The Virgin tells us that the People of God are refusing to carry out their mission, that of seeing to it that everything find its meaning in Jesus Christ. And she comes to tell us that this is a grave refusal.

## The Arm of Her Son

To bring home this truth, she again makes use of an eminently biblical image, the arm of her Son. The image shocks us. And yet, if we consult the Bible, we see that the arm of God is a saving arm. God saved his people "with mighty hand and outstretched arm" (Psalm 136:12a). In the New Testament Luke reports the words of Mary's Magnificat; the Lord "has shown might with his arm, dispersed the arrogant" (Luke 1:51). The mighty arm remains a saving arm. Mary at La Salette bears on her breast Christ crucified. The arm of her Son is this crucified arm, the supreme revelation of love for those who refuse to accept him.

Faced with this tragic situation, Mary speaks to us of her role as first believer and as Mother of the Church: "I am compelled to pray to him without ceasing." As she recalls the pains she takes for us, she cannot refrain from uttering a complaint, *"For how long a time do I suffer for you!"* Yes, she weeps, she prays, she takes pains, she suffers for her people. And she asks us in virtue of our baptism to take our place by her side. *"However much you pray, however much you do, you will never recompense the pains I have taken for you."* We are invited, as it were, to be like St. Paul, who wrote, "...in my flesh I am filling up what is lacking in the afflictions of Christ on behalf of his body, which is the church ..." (Colossians 1:24).

## The Seventh Day

Mary states precisely how we have rejected our mission as the People of God. She refers to the seventh day, on which it is stated in the Book of Genesis that "God ... rested ... from all the work he had undertaken" (Genesis 2:2).

The year 1846 marked the beginning of the industrial era. In the early coal mines, women and children under ten years of age worked all week long, up to twelve hours a day. So Our Lady reminds us that the seventh day is given so that we may cease from labor, not allowing ourselves to be brutalized by a hellish rhythm, but remembering that we are, above all, human beings created in the image of God and called to rise with Christ on the day destined to become the Christian sabbath, the Sunday of the resurrection. The current public debate regarding blue laws brings home to us all what is at stake in Mary's words.

## The Name of Her Son

And why does she next speak of the Name of her Son? Because, in that region, at that time, the neglect of Sunday Mass and the constant blaspheming by the cart drivers was a public manifestation of atheism. And the peasants understood this perfectly well.

Here again the Virgin brings us back to the Scriptures. In the prophet Ezekiel, among others, we find references to "my holy name" which they profaned among the nations (Ezekiel 36:20-23; see 20:8-14; 39:7). The Name of God, the Name revealed to Moses on Mount Sinai (Exodus 3), is blasphemed whenever human dignity is neglected.

In the New Testament Jesus was to receive "the Name that is above every name" (Philippians 2:9).

And in the Acts of the Apostles Peter declares: "There is no other name under heaven given to the human race by which we are to be saved" (Acts 4:12b). How is the name of God treated today? How many religious fanatics take turns killing each other in the name of God? What have we done to that divine name, rendered insignificant by our superficial and formalist religious practice?

## Looking at Events

Queen Victoria (1818-1901) painting from 1847 by Franz Xaver Winterhalter (1805-1873)

If one wished to sum up the beginning of Mary's message, one need only repeat the famous saying: "Do you desire the death of God? Well, then, look: the death of God is the death of humanity." In the rest of her message Mary will, in fact, invite us, to look at what is taking place around us. First the events of 1846, of course: the blighted harvest, the potato shortage. At Christmas, Father Mélin, the parish priest of Corps, wrote to his bishop to inform him that potatoes were not to be found any-

where, even at the price of gold. The following year the same would
be the case throughout Europe, especially in Ireland, **(1)** resulting in a
massive exodus towards the United States. In her annual discourse to
Parliament, Queen Victoria of England deplored the tragedy. Everywhere wheat, grapes and walnuts were either nowhere to be found
or were spoilt. The illustrious historian, Georges Duby, has detailed
this very serious agricultural crisis in terms which bear a remarkable
resemblance to Mary's very words. **(2)**

What is the point, today, of these observations made by the Blessed
Virgin in 1846? What are we doing to fight the widespread famine
which, in underdeveloped countries or nations at war, kills so many
human beings? What about the little children dying in such great
numbers in those countries? Fifteen million die every year according
to UNICEF. *"... and you pay no heed!"* When people lose their sense
of God, when they forget that God is our Father, human beings no
longer matter. No wonder Our Lady weeps and is so desperate to
warn us.

## Choosing Life

Accordingly, she invites us to draw the obvious conclusion—*"... if they
are converted"*—conversion! To rediscover an awareness of God. That
is basically what she came to request at La Salette: that we acknowl-
edge God's place—the first place—in our lives and rediscover our
sense of God's presence in every human being. The two are inseparable, for only then *"... the stones and rocks will become mounds of wheat,
and the potatoes will be self-sown in the fields."* This means that ways will
be found to deal with widespread famine in the Third World and thus
save our brothers and sisters who are dying of hunger. And once again
Mary's message sends us back to the Bible, to the Prophet Isaiah:
"Then the wolf shall be a guest of the lamb, and the leopard shall lie
down with the young goat; ... for the earth shall be filled with the
knowledge of the Lord, as water covers the sea" (11:6,9). In the New
Testament Jesus would say: "But seek first the kingdom [of God] ...
and all these things will be given you besides" (Matthew 6:33). All the
means which Mary proposes point toward this turning back first to
God, but likewise and inseparably to our brothers and sisters.

The wolf and the lamb by Wenceslaus Hollar (1607-1677);
photo: University of Toronto

# Prayer, Eucharist, Lent, Sending-Forth

First, prayer. *"Do you say your prayers well, my children?"* "Not very
well, Madame," Maximin and Melanie replied. The Blessed Virgin
well knows that we do not know how to pray, and we are very busy.
SO, she adds: *"When you cannot do better, say at least an Our Father and
a Hail Mary."* The *Our Father* is the essential Christian prayer which
Jesus taught us in the New Testament. The petition that the reign of
God may come is joined with the request that we be granted our daily bread and deliverance from evil. The *Hail Mary* enables us to live in
the company of the first among all believers.

She adds, *"... but when you have time, say more."* When will we have
the time? Where is the prayer of the People of God that our bishops
asked of us a few years ago? People bewail the fact that the Church
is in crisis. Where, then, is our prayer? Do we pray at all? We can ac-
complish nothing without prayer and an interior life. Genuine prayer
will not divert us from action. Pray we must; but we must also take
pains.

After speaking of prayer, Mary dwells on the Eucharist: *"There are none who go to Mass but a few somewhat elderly women.*" Deploring the abandonment of religious practice does little good. But would we be able to explain to an unbeliever or a young person what the Mass means to us? Do we ever discuss this with others? Is the Mass an integral part of our lives? The Council speaks of the Eucharist as "the source and summit" of the Christian life. We should become a Church which prays and celebrates, according to the desire of our bishops. Cardinal Marty, on a visit to La Salette, expressed it well: "It is an illusion to suppose we can persevere unless we are nourished with the Body given up for us and the Blood poured out for us."

Next comes a harsh word from the Blessed Virgin: *"During Lent they go to the meat market like dogs!"* "Intolerable", some may say; "such language is not worthy of Our Lady." And yet there are references to dogs in the New Testament (Matthew 7:6; 15:26; Mark 7:27). In speaking thus, is Mary perhaps trying to draw our attention to our sisters and brothers in the Third World, also her children, by helping us recover the true meaning of Lent? Lent is a time for sharing, through Operation Rice Bowl, etc., so that the neediest may become equal partners with us, but it is also an ascent towards Easter, towards the death and resurrection of Jesus.

Mary then concludes her discourse with an invitation to apostolic commitment. *"You will make this known to all my people."* She says it twice. The Gospel likewise ends with a sending-forth. If one has received good news, one cannot help wanting to share it with others. Are we aware that, by the very fact that we have been baptized and confirmed, we are all called to be apostles and missionaries? The Council reminded us of this.

Prayer, Eucharist, Lent, apostolic commitment—this may seem a rather austere message, too austere to express God's love. But is that love really absent here? Certainly not! Just before telling the children to make her message known, the Beautiful Lady asks a question; *"Have you never seen spoilt wheat, my children?"* This question seems out of place here. Mary seems to be repeating herself.

# God Present at the Heart of Our Lives

The terre du Coin (corner field) mentioned to Maximin by Our Lady of La Salette

To understand this part of the discourse, we need to go back to an event that transpired on September 20, 1846, when Pierre Selme brought Maximin back to his father, Monsieur Giraud. Even though it was a Sunday, he was not to be found at the church in Corps, but at the local pub. Selme related briefly the events of the preceding days. Roars of laughter greeted the news. Giraud's boy seeing the Blessed Virgin—that had to be the best joke of the year! Giraud was annoyed, and, once back home, he didn't want to hear any more of this nonsense. Finally, seeing the number of visitors intent on interviewing Maximin, he lost patience and threatened him, "Listen, either you are going to shut up or I will lock you up in the cellar with bread and water." But when Maximin looked at him and said timidly, "You know, papa, she spoke to me about you," he finally was willing to listen.

As Maximin told his story, his father remembered clearly that day in 1845 when he had gone to a farm at Coin, between two streams, the Drac and the Sézia, to buy an ash tree from the farmer. Before concluding the transaction, the farmer had brought him to his field and showed him his blighted wheat which fell into dust when the ears were rubbed together.

Giraud had not forgotten this, but up to this point there had been only one witness, the farmer. However, when on the way home, about a half-hour from Corps, he had given Maximin a piece of bread and said, *"Here, my child, eat some bread still this year,"* no one else had been there! He was sure of it. And now this man who, twenty years earlier, had closed the door on God in his life, was stunned to discover that this same God had never ceased for a single moment to be present to him. As a judge, rebuking him for not going to Mass on Sunday? No. Rather, here was a God who shared his anxiety as a father unable to provide bread for his son.

God is present in the life of each one of us—in all our own "farms of Coin."

But Giraud, a man of modern ideas, wanted to verify his son's account before admitting defeat. He sent his wife up the mountain to make sure Maximin wasn't making up stories. That was not quite enough, so he climbed the mountain himself after getting all the details from Maximin. He drank some of the water from the little spring and found himself cured of his asthma. This gave the coup de grace to his doubts and was the great moment of grace in his life.

When he returned to Corps that evening, he wanted to go to confession without delay. But his wife stopped him, "It's late, you can go tomorrow." And that is what he did first thing in the morning. Then he attended Mass and received Communion. He would do the same every day until the end of his life. He used to say, with a little smile, that he had to make up for all the times when he had missed Mass and had made his employees miss it by working on Sundays.

We need only remember this incident of Coin to understand the message of La Salette correctly, for here we learn from Our Lady how close God is to each one of us, like a Father full of tenderness. He is present to us individually, but also collectively.

We must place ourselves squarely among the People of God. We must discover the grace, the gift, the presence of God, who is more intimate to us than we are to ourselves, who shares our human life in its most ordinary realities, a God of love. The Virgin Mary weeps because we claim we can do without God's love and because this rejection on our part is grave, freighted with unbearable consequences. She cannot resign herself to this.

So she weeps, for she remains hopeful that we will return to the source of Life, to this God of infinite tenderness. That is what she came to tell us on September 19, 1846. And her people understood her. Spontaneously they began to invoke her as "the Reconciler of

Sinners." No one knows who gave her that title. It was born out of the faith of the People of God. It would soon be popularized by a confraternity of Our Lady Reconciler. And to this day that title remains the key to understanding the Beautiful Lady of La Salette. But we will reflect on this in greater depth in the course of this book.

# The Face of God in the Message

## The Discretion of the 'One Who Cannot be Named'

The word "God" is never used in the message of La Salette. That may seem strange to us; after all, why did Mary come to La Salette if not to invite us to return to the Lord our God?

Perhaps it is good for us to let ourselves be surprised and to allow Mary to guide us towards an increasingly appreciated attitude nowadays, namely, discretion, reserve.

"You shall not take the name of the Lord, your God, in vain" (Exodus 20:7a). How that divine name has been misused, devalued, abused throughout history! The conduct of certain ayatollahs or other religious funda-

The face of God in the Creation of Adam by Michelangelo (1475-1584) in Sistine Chapel ceiling

mentalists who consider it their duty to kill you in God's name, calls to mind what the Crusaders did in Albigensian and Palestinian lands. And what about the *Gott mit uns (God with us)* on the belts of German soldiers, or the *"In God we trust"* on American dollars? Is not this also a profanation of God's name?

Faced with all these unbearable, constantly recurring excesses, Mary gives us the example of a rigorous respect for God's mystery. This is something our secularized society needs. Emmanuel Mounier condensed it into a striking formula: "Trifle not with God in pursuit of your whims only to put him on later like a poultice to soothe you." This contemporary imperative also squares with traditional theology which has always taught that, in speaking of God words are never adequate. Every genuine theology, when it has said all it has to say, humbly recognizes that it cannot really say anything at all about God. The Virgin of La Salette evidences that discretion with respect to the use of God's name, but this obviously does not prevent her from taking an original approach in teaching us how to meet God.

## At the Field of Coin

When she asked Maximin and Melanie whether they had ever seen spoiled wheat, the question might at first seem of no importance and superfluous. Why, before taking her leave of the children, return to the subject of spoiled wheat? The fact is that her recalling this incident was to be, for the wheelwright Giraud, his road to Damascus. For many years he had not set foot in church. He typifies all agnostics who have seen too much to remain believers. And his first reaction on hearing of his son's strange adventure was that of complete skepticism and his set refusal to listen to him.

But when, at wits' end, Maximin told him that the Beautiful Lady had spoken about him, he finally condescended to listen. And he was completely overpowered. He remembered clearly the spoiled wheat which had crumbled in his hands, and the piece of bread he had given to his son when they were only half an hour's distance from Corps. His words, repeated exactly, could not have been heard by anyone else; of that he was certain, for he had been alone with Maximin.

This changed everything. And immediately, abruptly, but also with infinite tenderness, that Presence which he thought he could do without, prevailed over him. "You know when I sit and stand … with all my ways you are familiar. Even before a word is on my tongue, Lord, you know it all. Behind and before you encircle me and rest your hand upon me." These words of Psalm 139:2-5 express the lived experience of Mr. Giraud, his discovery of God's true face. This was not a judgmental God ready to punish his religious indifference, but a God present in his life and attentive to the whole reality of his human existence. God had seen the spoiled wheat and shared the anxiety of a father humiliated at not having any more bread to give his child.

This is the God revealed to Moses in the Book of Exodus: "I have witnessed the affliction of my people in Egypt and have heard their cry against their taskmasters, so I know well what they are suffering. There-fore, I have come down to rescue

The window in the La Salette Basilica depicting Maximin and his father in the terre du Coin (corner field)

them from the power of the Egyptians ... Now, go! I am sending you ..." (Exodus 3:7-8a,10a).

The New Testament in turn confirms that God is indeed the atten-tive witness of our lives here on earth. John writes: "Philip found Nathanael and told him, 'We have found the one about whom Moses wrote in the Law, and also the prophets, Jesus, son of Joseph, from Nazareth.' But Nathanael said to him, 'Can anything good come from Nazareth?' Philip said to him, 'Come and see.' Jesus saw Nathanael coming toward him and said of him, 'Here is a true Israelite. There is no duplicity in him.' Nathanael said to him, 'How do you know me?' Jesus answered and said to him, 'Before Philip called you, I saw you under the fig tree.' Nathanael answered him, 'Rabbi, you are the Son of God; you are the King of Israel'" (John 1:45-49).

The God of the Coin farm is none other than this God who sees and hears the misery of people and wants to deliver them from it. It is the God of Jesus Christ whom the astonished Nathanael discovered in turn. It is not the God of philosophers and scholars, but, as Pascal would say, "the God who is sensitive to hearts." That was the God Gi-raud discovered. How could he not undertake a radical change of life?

# A God Passionately in Love with Humanity

The God of biblical Revelation is a passionate lover of humankind. So is the God of La Salette: a God who wants to speak to people through the landmark events of their lives. This is so true that some have criticized Mary's message as crassly materialistic. Who is this Lady who speaks of the potato harvest and blighted wheat, of walnuts going bad and grapes rotting? And what is this business of stones and rocks changing into mounds of wheat, and potatoes sowing themselves?

Materialistic language? In that case we should take the whole Bible to task for being materialistic! What, in fact, are the main topics addressed in Sacred Scripture? Eating, drinking, clothing oneself, building one's house, increasing one's flock, cultivating one's vines, fig trees and grain: all these things, then and now, constitute the basis of *economic life*. Here we see the economy in its most rudimentary form, of course, but it was no less constraining in the past than it is today.

Again, the Bible speaks to us about *family life*, about marriage, about wives and husbands, about rivalries and jealousies, about adultery and prostitution, rape and incest, alongside moving examples of fidelity in a unique, fully requited love. Different ways of life are also mentioned: tribal life, slavery, invasion of national territory, exile, conquests, insurrections. Hence the Bible is a witness to the long *polit-*

*Vatican Council II* by **Ernani Costantini (1922-2007), Church of Saints Quiricus and Julietta, Italy**

26

*ical history* of a people. That history, with all its diverse accounts and literary forms-poetic works, wisdom books, historical epics, makes up the cultural expression of this people.

In the above enumeration of biblical topics, one can easily recognize the chapter headings of Vatican II's, *"Constitution on the Church in the Modern World (Gaudium et spes)"*, part two. A century before that Council, Mary had already come to tell us, at La Salette, about this God whom we can encounter nowhere else but in the realities of economic, family, political, cultural and international life. And again, like the Bible, Mary is attentive both to the lives of individuals and to the life of the community. The Bible recounts the lives of individual persons, with names, faces and personalities; with their qualities and defects, their greatness and pettiness. We have only to reflect on the engaging character of King David. In the same way, Mary shows us a God who is personally involved in the life of the wheelwright Giraud.

Yet the Bible never loses sight of the collective aspect of the destiny each individual is living out. David is never viewed separately from his people, nor his people from the surrounding nations. In the same way, Mary addresses herself to Mr. Giraud, to the region of Corps and all her people; and the conversion she asks for is of course personal, but likewise collective. *"If they are converted"*, she says.

Hence the Virgin of La Salette is no more materialistic than the Bible and the Council Fathers who believe that the meeting of God and humanity takes place at the heart of earthly realities. As the biblical God, so the God of La Salette addresses people personally and collectively, at the heart of world events, for it is there, and nowhere else, that the dialogue between the divine and the human is engaged. *"It is all on your account and you take no heed of it."* Do we not find here the insight underlying the approach of Catholic Action: to cast the events of our human lives in faith terms, in order to discern in them the signs of the presence and activity of God?

# God Recognized in Everyday Events

What the Blessed Virgin says at La Salette constitutes a reading of the events of 1846 from the perspective of faith. To be more easily convinced of this, please see the article by Georges Duby. (2) Reading this text, we realize how deeply Mary's message is rooted in the events of this period. The Virgin does not offer a political, economic or cultural reading of events, as a journalist could have done, as indeed historians do today. Hers is a faith-view, after the manner of the prophets who strove to discover in events the signs of God's call to personal and collective conversion. In the message of La Salette, the life of faith is not a life set apart any more than it is in the Bible. Dialogue with God, indeed, must begin with all those events, those of the most ordinary life, through which God graciously chooses to reveal himself to us.

## God Revealed in Jesus Christ

In her message, not once does Mary mention God. On the other hand, six times she uses the expression "my Son", and that is significant. She well knows that it is the face of Jesus, her Son, that has allowed human beings to know God definitively. The entire Old Testament was only a long divine preparation and a long human search for this definitive revelation.

People in the Bible progressed in the knowledge of God because *they were able to speak to God about their concerns as human beings.* It was not by an accumulation of abstract reflections that they grew in their faith in God. It was by conversing with God about all that pertained to their life. In the course of this dialogue they came to speak God's own language. Indeed, this revelation was to culminate in Jesus Christ, truly divine and truly human.

After Jesus Christ was born in Palestine, it would be from human lips that the living Word of God was proclaimed. What was lisped by the lips of his people throughout its long history would now be spoken in its perfection by the lips of Christ. For the man called Jesus was also the Word of God, the utterance of God. Jesus knew God with a knowledge that was full and perfect, the very knowledge with which God knows himself. In Christ God finally revealed who he really is—not a God who is witness and judge, observer of human life, but the true God, fully involved in human affairs, a God fully committed to our human destiny. God shares in the whole reality of this destiny. What gives joy to people gives joy to God. What is a source of human suffering causes suffering in God? God suffers and dies in the man Jesus Christ. Mary's entire message tells us that human suffering causes suffering for the God who can bear neither the death of little children nor the great famine.

At La Salette, as at the conclusion of biblical revelation, the human vision of God is purified. It is God the ineffable one, the inaccessible one, the incomprehensible one, whose name is not even spoken, but likewise it is the God who is close to people, who speaks to them about their life and concerns, God made flesh in Jesus Christ, the Son. Mary makes known to us a God who is in search of humankind, who knows people in a committed, loving, down-to-earth way, a God who, in Jesus Christ, has entered marriage with the human race. Our Lady's message is for us a testimony to the passionate love God bears us. In her view, we can be nothing less than God's partners.

## In Jesus Christ Crucified

This passionate love of God blazes out in a very particular manner on the cross. It is the high point of biblical revelation; it is likewise the high point of the message of La Salette: the luminous crucifix she bears on her heart. That had been the brightest thing, the source of all the light which dazzled Maximin and Melanie before it embraced them. And then there were Mary's tears, also made of light. At La Salette, as in the Bible, the ulti-

*Christ and the Good Thief*
by Titian (1490-1576)

mate revelation of the face of God is the face of Jesus, the Suffering Servant and the Risen One.

# A Menacing God who Resorts to Blackmail?

It is impossible to ask oneself about the face of God as presented in the message without taking into account two expressions pilgrims to La Salette often find disconcerting. First of all, God's dialogue with humanity in the concrete events is presented to us as a sort of bargaining. The alternative is conditional: *"If my people will not submit, I shall be forced to let fall ..."* whereas, *"if they are converted, the stones and rocks will be changed into heaps of wheat."* Isn't this kind of blackmail totally unbecoming?

But this objection could be raised against the Bible itself. We read in Deuteronomy: "I set before you here, this day, a blessing and a curse: a blessing for obeying the commandments of the Lord, your God, which I give you today; a curse if you do not obey the commandments of the Lord, your God ..." (Deuteronomy 11:26-28a). Chapter 30 proposes a very similar text: "See, I have today set before you, life and good, death and evil. If you obey the commandments of the Lord, your God, ... loving the Lord ... and walking in his ways, ... you will live ... If, however, your heart turns away and you do not obey, ... you will certainly perish ... I call heaven and earth today to witness against you: I have set before you, life and death, the blessing and the curse. *Choose life, then*, that you and your descendants may live, by loving the Lord, your God, obeying his voice, and holding fast to him. For that will mean life for you ..." (Deuteronomy 30:15-20a). The parallel between Our Lady's message and the Bible is absolutely striking. Should we therefore reject them both? Would it not be a better idea to take a closer look at them?

These texts of Deuteronomy date back to Jeremiah and the religious reform undertaken by King Josiah in 622 BC. To carry out this reform, great stress was laid on the Book of the Law discovered in the temple. This Book bears witness to, and is the consequence of, the experience of the people of God. In the long history of the seekers of God, fidelity to God proved to be the source of life while infidelity was the source of death. The Virgin invites us to verify that truth today. What is the result of the desire to build a world in which men and women are the sole masters, a world without reference to God?

Is it not a world of great famines and infant mortality? At that point, either we turn to the living God, acknowledging the dynamics of the divine within ourselves, or we will turn away and imprison ourselves in the blind alleys of a world in despair.

Every situation we experience places this choice before us—for or against the Lord. Our future is in the balance. This option is in keeping with our human destiny and it underlines the mystery of our human freedom vis-a-vis God's freedom. Humanity's true greatness appears in our call to enter into a free partnership with God.

## The Arm of My Son

The second difficulty that pilgrims grapple with relates to Our Lady's statement about her Son's arm which she can no longer withhold. This expression has often been noted and by a contemporary theologian, the author of some remarkable writings on Christ and God. In one of his books, he speaks of "the strange doctrine concerning the Christ of La Salette whom the compassionate and merciful Virgin implores not to punish." **(3)** One must first note that Mary's message does not speak of punishment even once. At La Salette we are not dealing with that inexorable Christ one contemplates in the Sistine Chapel, a Christ whose wrath the Virgin is supposedly charged with appeasing. That Christ is not the Christ of the New Testament, the Risen One now seated at the right hand of the Father, whom the Letter to the Hebrews definitively declares to be our intercessor with the Father (Hebrews 9:24).

"The arm of my Son" in the House Chapel in Hartford, CT

On the other hand, like Mary at La Salette, the Bible often speaks to us of the arm of God. But it is always a saving arm. God saves his people "with strong hand and outstretched arm" (Deuteronomy 4:34b).

At the threshold of the New Testament, Mary, in her Magnificat, sums up the entire Old Testament by speaking to us of a God who "has shown might with his arm, and dispersed the arrogant" (Luke 1:51a).

The image of God's arm is an unmistakable image of biblical Revelation. Mary directs our attention to it and warns us that the arm of her Son weighs heavily on the proud who refuse to submit. This arm speaks to us of the passionate and jealous love of God for all. God cannot be resigned to seeing the human family suffer the heavy consequences of its refusal, namely, spoiled wheat, famine, the death of little children. When Mary hints at her Son's abandoning her people, it is because of her people's abandoning her Son. She speaks of a God who can tolerate neither alternative. This image of her Son's arm reveals to us the tragic mystery of the rejection of the Savior's love. Certain texts of the New Testament say the same. "Depart from me ... For I was hungry, and you gave me no food ... What you did not do for one of these least ones, you did not do for me." (Matthew 25:41b,45b). And the Letter to the Romans speaks to us of the "The wrath of God ... being revealed from heaven" and those who suppress the truth by their wickedness (see Romans 1:18a-32).

Gabriel-Marie-Joseph Matagrin (1919-2004), Bishop of Grenoble

"The God of love is always revealed as torn between anger and mercy, which are the two faces of the unique passion of God for humankind", writes Gabriel-Marie-Joseph Matagrin (1919-2004), Bishop of Grenoble, in his preface to Jean Stern's book **(4)**, before citing Origen at length. This passionate God suffers at being excluded from the lives of men and women through neglect or rejection. Jesus Christ likewise is passionate about those who refuse his love. An impasse has apparently been reached between the love God is offering and the people's refusal to respond.

But this tragic confrontation is not insurmountable. The arm which weighs upon the people is revealed as a saving arm, for it is that of the Suffering Servant, of him whose crucified and luminous image Mary bears on her heart. Mary is not content with speaking of the arm she can no longer withhold. She further shows us that arm nailed to the Cross. It is in the passion of the Crucified One, of the Suffering Servant, that she reveals to us the arm of her Son as a saving arm.

Isaiah 53:1 asks, "To whom has the arm of the Lord been revealed?" We find the answer a few verses further on in 53:8: "Seized and condemned, [the Suffering Servant] was taken away," and in 53:5a: "he was ... crushed for our iniquity"; and 53:6: "The Lord laid upon him the guilt of us all." This link established in Isaiah 53 between the revelation of the saving arm and the sufferings of the Servant is exactly the link Mary suggests to us, in speaking of the arm of her Son, and in showing us the crucified arm of Jesus whom she bears on her heart. It is this Christ crucified, the Suffering Servant, who is able to transform the power to refuse that human malice inspires into the power of a superabundant life.

Isaiah 53 seems to be where we should look to find the meaning of the arm, since Chapter 12 of John's Gospel also makes the same comparison between the people's rejection of Jesus and his paschal sacrifice which again reveals God's saving arm. We begin to understand how deep is the revelation of God's face which the Virgin presents in speaking of the arm of her Son. This image reveals a God passionately in love with us, the Father who goes so far as to allow his Son to die in order to reveal to us that love which is stronger than all our refusals.

Mary, at La Salette, does not claim to take upon herself Jesus' role as sole mediator before the Father. On the other hand, though she withholds the arm of her Son, she shows us that humans are called to co-operate in the task of reconciliation the Suffering Servant accomplished. Mary at La Salette reminds us that she cooperated with her Son before us. *"I am compelled to pray to him without ceasing. what pains I have taken for you! How long a time do I suffer for you!"* And she challenges us in turn to accept our part in this task: *"However much you pray, however much you do, you will never recompense the pains I have taken for you."*

If her people are no longer the People of God, they weigh down the arm of her Son, they are heading towards death, they doom the world to death, to the wrath of God (Romans 2:4-8). But if they once again become the People of God, if they submit to Jesus Christ, they will live and give life to the universe.

Mary is the perfect icon of this People of God which is no longer the object of wrath but is now a partner in the reconciliation of the world. It is her entire people who should feel compelled to pray, to act and even to suffer with her, so that this world may no longer be a sign of divine wrath, but of God's tenderness regained (Romans 5:1-11).

## Continuing, with Mary, to Speak of God in Today's World

Handout printed in 1850 in Epinal in northeastern France

At La Salette Mary teaches us to speak of God to all people. What we have difficulty doing, she accomplishes admirably in her message. And her people have understood her, for she found a way to speak of God not only in a language accessible to all, but also in God's own words—those of Sacred Scripture and those of her Son. She spoke to us of a God who wants to enter into partnership with humanity, even as the latter tragically dares to reject love.

Today, as in 1846, our world awaits a word of commitment. It has no use for polite talk. It must be made aware of God's passionate love.

# -3-
# Reconciliation Today

There is a famous prayer of Abbé Perreyve which begins, "Virgin Mary, in the midst of your days of glory, do not forget the sorrows of earth."

Clearly, the pilgrim who contemplates the weeping Mother is convinced that Mary has never forgotten the sorrows of this world. No long discourses are needed to prove it. Still, this sight of Mary in tears, and even more so, her words: *"For how long a time do I suffer for you,"* continue to shock people.

Eminent theologians have asked themselves how it could be possible for the Virgin Mary, living, sharing the glory of the resurrection, to suffer. I do not know whether we will ever adequately answer this question, but what is certain is that this image of Mary can enable us to enter very practically into the mystery

Abbé Henri Perreyve
(1831-1865),
a French Catholic priest,
professor and theologian

of reconciliation. Mary, in the definitive joy of the Father, wants for nothing, yet she cannot reconcile herself to a happy life without others.

She wants to be fully involved in the dramas her children live in this world. That undoubtedly is the deep source of the attraction men and women have always felt towards Our Lady of La Salette. Under her guidance, we will have no trouble discovering the salient features of this mystery of reconciliation.

## A Subversive Word

Let us first observe that the word "reconciliation" is rejected by many people today. It is perceived as subversive. How are we supposed to believe in the need for activism and the struggle for justice and, at the same time speak of reconciliation? It is important to note that Mary does not use the word in her message at La Salette. But she lives the reality to the full, by situating herself at the heart of the dramas and struggles which are the inevitable lot of our humanity. Mary presents herself as a credible witness of reconciliation.

Far from ignoring human sufferings and trials, she makes them the raw material of her people's spiritual adventure. Mary experienced to the depth of her being the anguish of the men and women of 1846 who saw their wheat fall into dust, the potatoes spoiling, the walnuts and grapes rotting. Mary cannot bear to see people starving. And she knows only too well from experience how excruciating and unbearable it is to hold one's dead child in one's arms.

Contemporary historians emphasize the extent to which the agricultural crisis of 1845-46 fueled financial speculation and describe all the conflicts caused by the crisis, culminating in France in the revolution of 1848. At La Salette, therefore, Mary draws our attention to the tragedies and conflicts of that period, and bids us use them as a starting point in finding the way of reconciliation.

## 1—Immersed in the struggle:

If we wish to be credible believers, our first step will not consist in giving a lecture on reconciliation. Rather we must resolutely immerse ourselves in the struggles involving the fate of peoples of our own times. Towards that end we, like Mary in 1846, must look clearly at the world, starting with our own life. We must constantly overcome our blindness and open our eyes to today's tragedies and injustices. Now and again we will need to revise our analysis of the situation. We will look back at two analyses, already dated no doubt, but overall still relevant. In 1982 the Annual World Report on the Economic System and Planning (5) stated the following:

–"Nearly everywhere, and in spite of many persevering efforts, *hunger and poverty continue to increase* and are making headway even in European countries.

–"In many countries, *power is in the hands of the rich*, the military, party leaders, technocrats, while it eludes the people, the majority. In those countries the influence of the poor, the downtrodden and the humble is decreasing while the number of ethnic groups whose freedom and creativity are scoffed at is rising.

–"Those who possess *information*-and often power as well are rarely willing to share either. Social pressures unite in making people into simple executors of decisions taken elsewhere, to the point where they find life meaningless and see their culture annihilated.

–"*The race for wealth, knowledge and power, often at the price of crushing others, makes human beings into objects*, reducing them just to their economic function as producers and consumers, and kills values such as friendship, a sense of celebration, poetry, prayer ...

–"*The waste in military spending* (a million dollars per minute for armaments throughout the world) is on the increase along with the risk of an apocalypse. These resources could be used to develop a peaceful world in which people could live truly human lives.

–"*A new, anarchic international order* is being created, often by force, whereby the opening of new markets in countries able to pay import duties is more important than providing food for the hungry, drink for the thirsty, care for the sick and shelters for the homeless ... "

Pope John Paul II visits Bosnia and Herzegovina in 1997; photo: CNS

Another analysis was made by Pope John Paul II in his encyclical, *Sollicitudo rei socialis*, in 1987:

–The Pope, in his overview of the contemporary world, observes the "persistence and widening of the gap between the developed North and the developing South of the planet." Less advanced countries come to a point where they find their progress seriously impeded.

Due to illiteracy and the lack of higher education, and because of all kinds of discrimination, particularly racism, many people in poor countries are prevented from participating in their own development. Do we not have "a too narrow, too exclusively economic conception of development"?

–Three disorders pose very serious questions for the international community—refugees, terrorism, and demographics.

–The Pope then highlights three signs of warped development throughout the world:

    1. the housing crisis due to increasing urbanization;

    2. unemployment and under-employment;

    3. the international debt: the credit intended to promote development has only slowed it down, or even caused further underdevelopment.

We must denounce the existence of economic, financial and social mechanisms which ensure that some remain rich while others remain poor.

## Jesus Christ Betrayed

For any Christian who wishes to be credible, this hard look at our world is indispensable. In fact, half of the world's Christians live in the wealthiest fourth of the planet - to which I and most of my readers belong. And Christians comprise only five percent of the poorest twenty-five percent of humanity. The rich countries, where Christians live, are the ones who set too low the price of products bought from poor nations and block international negotiations. All this contradicts the *Magnificat* (Luke 1 :52-53), the account of the last judgment (Matthew 25:32-46), the narrative of the passion of Jesus who became poor (2 Corinthians 8:9) without grasping at the rank which made him equal to God (Philippians 2:6) and accepted death on a cross of infamy (Philippians 2:8). Pagan peoples will have to look elsewhere for hope. Christians living in poor countries question the sincerity of the Church. And the youth in our rich countries can only tum away from a faith which has become irrelevant and incapable of sharing in the transformation of the world.

*The first indispensable step towards a process of reconciliation* is, therefore, to *take personal responsibility*, in one way or another, for *the many devastating conflicts in our world*. There is no escaping this. It is imperative that Christians leave behind the excessive individualism of our paganized world: me, my career, my success, my wealth-look out for number one. It is not a question of struggling just for one's own freedom, but we must struggle for the freedom of all. Look about you: "You are a human being, you are in pain. I share your pain, so let us fight together that together we may be cured of your pain which has become mine", as Abbé Pierre expressed it. That is the first step in a reconciliation process. It is Mary's first step at La Salette. She takes into account the sufferings of her people as well as her own. She invites us to a collective undertaking because she is concerned with the sufferings of her people. And in the midst of her suffering people she likewise suffers: *"For how long a time do I suffer for you!"*

## 2—Believing nonetheless:

But perhaps one may be tempted to give up, to become discouraged at the prospect of such a vast and seemingly impossible task. What's the use? Worse still, a believer may be beset with doubts. When one views the state of the world and reads reports like those cited above, is not one tempted to lose faith in a God of love, the Lord of human history? To borrow an expression of Abbé Pierre, we have to be *believers nonetheless*.

Our Lady of La Salette by Mrs. Roskos, Marietta, GA; used with permission

In the face of all the horrible evils in the world, the great famine and the death of little children, Mary at La Salette teaches us to become *believers nonetheless*. There is an image of Mary which we do not probably meditate on enough, namely of the Blessed Virgin wearing heavy chains around her shoulders, chains which—as the children testified—seemed to crush her.

## Mary's Chains

As we contemplate this image of Mary in chains, we can perhaps come to understand who God is. God is not an all-powerful master of the universe. If that were the case, we would be justified in condemning God for permitting so much evil in the world. Haven't we too often called God to account? How often have we not blamed God for the world's ills? As Mary said at La Salette, *"You swore, you took the name of my Son in vain."* She came to show us on the contrary that these evils occur *"all on your account."* She does not throw this in our face to make us feel guilty, but she does want to emphasize our freedom and our responsibility. It is not God who is the source of misery in the world. Human beings, with their God-given freedom, are responsible for its creation.

## A Captive God

God cannot infringe on this human freedom. The idea of an almighty, autocratic God is only a caricature. Almighty, yes, but *the captive Almighty*, so respectful of human freedom as to be enchained by it. God is the all-powerful one who has chosen to become a captive of love. And the heavy chains on Mary's shoulders at La Salette are a striking revelation of this truth. It is not mere words, or a hollow discourse; it is the commitment of the first among believers. Mary in chains is the very image of God the omnipotent captive. And it is not only her chains that testify to this, but likewise the crucifix she bears on her breast.

"When I look upon Christ on the cross", to quote Abbé Pierre once again, "I see all the suffering of humanity, and in his nailed hands, I see the Almighty made captive, a willing captive of our God-given freedom."

## Christ the Reconciler

Thus, it is that Mary at La Salette teaches us to become *believers, none-*

*theless.* By her chains, by her crucifix, she shows us who God really is. God is her Son who demonstrates his solidarity with all the suffering of the world, enduring suffering in order to combat suffering. This same Son who as God is the captive of our freedom. She shows us to what extent God loves us. She shows us the one Reconciler, the one who "took away our infirmities and bore our diseases" (from Matthew 8:17, cited in Isaiah 53:4a). She shows us a God who loves to that extent, a God in whom we can believe, in spite of all the evil in the world.

Because God loves to that extent, we can be *believers nonetheless*; this is a second step on the way of reconciliation. We must not only assume our share of responsibility for the misery of the world, but also live as *believers nonetheless*. And this second step represents the original and irreplaceable contribution of Christians in the immense field of human struggle. For we know for certain that the God enchained by our love will let love have the last word. Despite the prospect of ultimate struggles which never seem to end, we know that love crucified will have the last word. Reconciliation has already been acquired for us, it is a gift, to be received, to be accepted. By becoming *believers nonetheless*, we become carriers of this beneficial virus of reconciliation in the midst of the world's struggles.

### 3—Witnesses of the eternal in time:

Thank God, many are those who have given themselves generously to the struggle against the disorders of the world. Among them, Christians are neither the first nor the majority, as John Paul II and others have observed with sorrow. We must therefore join these men and women on many fields of combat. But we will have our own manner of living that struggle. Like the rest, we will keep our eyes wide open to the horrors of the world, but we will also be bearers of what Abbé Pierre calls "contagious enlightenment: to demonstrate that life is a little bit of time in which we learn to love forever."

Because we are *believers nonetheless*, we can testify to our vision of humanity. Human life always entails two aspects—the one is visible in the duration of time, while the other is invisible, beyond time, eternal. *To reveal, to manifest this twofold dimension of human existence, is the third component of the Christian undertaking of reconciliation.* "In you, O Lord, our human work receives the stamp of eternity," according to the words of a French hymn. It is essential that we never separate the provisional, time-bound dimension of human struggles from their definitive dimension in eternity. We can truly be Christian artisans of reconciliation only if we never dissociate these two dimensions.

## Possible Failure and Certainty Nevertheless

But we must entertain no illusion. No one can guarantee that human struggles will infallibly lead to tomorrows bursting with song. There is no guarantee that we will succeed in conquering famine, arms stockpiling, and totalitarianism. It is not certain that we will attain a democracy where rich and poor have equal rights. It is not true to say that we will definitely achieve a new international economic order that is bound to be satisfactory. The world's future, because of us, may yet be a nuclear holocaust. And how often has it not happened that those who struggled against oppression have in turn become oppressors. Hence to promise that our struggles here on earth will end in victory is a lie.

Faith, however, assures us of one thing: beyond our questionable historical successes, the human enterprise bears a dimension that is rooted in history's moment but that is to be fully unveiled only in the moment beyond time.

## A Tough Balancing Act

This does not mean we should take refuge in an imaginary and subversive hereafter, "detachment from earth and the desire for heaven." If Christians detach themselves from the world's struggles and action and seek asylum in the hereafter, they can no longer be credible believers. They are no longer the disciples of the God made flesh in Jesus Christ and they certainly are not acting in accord with Mary's message at La Salette.

But neither can they limit their horizon to purely earthly struggles. On the one hand, they would risk experiencing bitter disillusionment, and on the other, they would betray their unique mission, that of bearing witness to the dimension of eternity, beyond the setbacks and victories of human struggles. And here they can be sure of the success of God's reconciling work, at least for all those who willingly accept it. From this point of view the span of human life which is given to us is a time of apprenticeship in the love that conquers evil, in reconciling love.

## Rooted in the Gospel

Many pages of the Gospel emphasize this presence of eternity in time. Let us take one of them, the scene of the last judgment in Matthew's Gospel: "Lord, when did we see you hungry and feed you, or thirsty and give you drink? When did we see you a stranger and welcome you, or naked and clothe you? When did we see you ill or in prison, and visit you?" (Matthew 25:37b-39). All those who have taken part in our human struggles to reconcile humanity will live this surprising moment when the eternal dimension of their human acts is revealed to them, whether their good intentions achieved complete success or not. And then will come the stunning revelation: "Amen, I say to you, whatever you did for one of these least brothers of mine, you did for me" (Matthew 25:40b). And this revelation will be no less stunning in the opposite sense, for all those who remained indifferent to human struggles: "Amen, I say to you, what you did not do for one of these least ones, you did not do for me" (Matthew 25:45b).

## Re-echoed at La Salette

At La Salette Mary emphasizes this profound link between time and eternity in calling us to conversion. *"If they are converted,"* she tells us, *"the stones and rocks will be changed into mounds of wheat and the pota- toes will be self-sown in the land."* Mary then emphasizes the theological dimension of conversion, its aspect of communion with eternity, urging us to pray morning and evening, to pray more, to take part in the Sunday eucharist without mocking at religion, to share with others during Lent and to give our lives an apostolic thrust. But before emphasizing this dimension, she invites us to make her concern about the great famine and the death of little children and the creation of those indispensable mounds of wheat and potatoes our own. It is her way of telling us clearly that we must never separate what God has joined together in the eternal depth of our human history. And if Mary came to weep at La Salette, was it not to call Christians to take up again their mission of "contagious enlightenment", to borrow Abbé Pierre's expression once more?

## Reconciliation is Crucial!

On May 31, 1980, Pope John Paul II celebrated Mass at the church of Saint-Denis on the outskirts of Paris, with the working class. He chose that day to preach on the words of the *Magnificat*: "He has shown might with his arm, dispersed the arrogant of mind and heart. He has thrown down the rulers from their thrones but lifted up the lowly. The hungry he has filled with good things; the rich he has sent away empty" (Luke 1:51-53).

The pope put this question to his audience:

> "In the name of what right ... have this willingness to fight for the truth and this hunger and thirst for justice come to be systematically dissociated from the words of the Mother of God? By what right has the struggle for justice in the world come to be linked to a program of radical denial of God, to an organized program of atheistic indoctrination of individuals and societies? That is a question we must ask ourselves."

It is imperative that Christians raise that question and actively commit themselves to the struggle of today's men and women for a renewed, reconciled world. It is imperative that Christians become *believers nonetheless*, willing, in union with the Virgin of La Salette, to allow themselves to be enchained by that eternal love which became flesh in human time.

# -4-
# Come Near, My Children!

Come near, my children, in bronze by Brother Juan Magro Andres, M.S. (1928-2008)

"Bah! You expect me to believe that this little one has seen the Blessed Virgin, and she doesn't even say her prayers!" Thus exclaimed, on the evening of September 19, 1846, the youngest son of old Maman Pra in their dwelling at Les Ablandins when, after the children had told their story, his mother told him not to work on Sundays any more. His remark made perfect sense. Who besides Mary would have chosen the likes of Maximin and Melanie for the challenging mission of transmitting her message to all her people?

## Two Poor, Unfit Children

Melanie, a frail girl, did not look her age. Born on November 7, 1831, she was, however, 15 years old. For several years already, she had been deprived of her parents' affection. The family was so poor that she was "sold"—the local expression for hired out—to the farms in the vicinity of Corps as a shepherdess, at Sainte-Luce, Quet-en-Beaumont, and finally in 1846 at Les Ablandins.

Maximin was younger, born on August 27, 1835, in Corps, also to a poor family. His mother had died and the woman who became his step-mother when Giraud remarried was also to die young, soon after the apparition. Neither of the children ever attended school or catechism classes. They had to wait till the second Sunday of Easter,

45

1848 to be allowed to make their first Communion. Hence both had thus far had an unsettled life. They were unfit a priori, and yet it was indeed to them that Our Lady extended her invitation, "Come near, my children!"

## God's Ways

But let us suppose that it was precisely because of their instability that they were chosen. There is nothing surprising in this for anyone who knows anything at all about biblical revelation. "Not as mortals see does God see, because mortals see the appearance but the Lord looks into the heart", God said to the prophet Samuel whom he had appointed to choose a king for his people. None of the seven sons of Jesse was to be chosen. (11) Then Samuel asked Jesse, 'Are these all the sons you have?' Jesse replied, 'There is still the youngest, but he is tending the sheep.' Samuel said to Jesse, "Send for him; ... Jesse had the young man brought to them. He was ruddy, a youth with beautiful eyes, and good looking. The Lord said: There—anoint him, for this is the one!" (1 Samuel 16:7,11-12).

We will of course encounter this privileged place of little ones in the New Testament in St. Paul's writings: "Consider your own calling, brothers. Not many of you were wise by human standards ... ; God chose the foolish of the world to shame the wise, those who count for nothing, to reduce to nothing those who are something" (1 Corinthians 1:26a,28).

## An Astonishing Ability

Those who are skeptical about the reality of the apparition of La Salette will find such use of scripture texts a little too convenient. There is some truth to that, considering that neither Maximin nor Melanie was ever canonized, or likely to be. Nevertheless, untold numbers of people have accepted the word of these two poor children and the Church has judged that they were "neither deceivers nor deceived." Marie des Brulais, in her *Journal d'une institutrice* and the Abbé Dupanloup, far more demanding than she, were both astounded at the quality of the children's witnessing. While their external demeanor left much to be desired, whenever the apparition was discussed they amazed their interviewers by their wisdom and their ability to elude the most subtly laid traps.

There would be much to say about their lives after the apparition, but we will leave that to others. Briefly, however, we can mention their fidelity in bearing witness to the "Beautiful Lady."

In 1875 Maximin, on his death bed, made a solemn profession of faith in the truth of the Apparition. And Melanie, in her seventies, once again told the story on that very same mountain, early in the twentieth century. She died in 1904.

Bishop Felix Dupanloup (1802-1878); photo: François-Marie Gobinet de Villecholle

Theirs was a rather difficult life. Why? Perhaps because they came from among the poor, those we call today the underclass, who can rise above their poverty only with great difficulty. "Blessed are you who are poor, for the kingdom of God is yours" (Luke 6:20b). For Mary at La Salette, as also for Jesus in the Gospel, children and the poor are God's favorite people.

# Do Not Be Afraid

*The Annunciation*: **An Oil Painting by Fra Angelico (circa 1395 –1455)**

*"Come near, my children. do not be afraid. I am here to tell you great news."* These are the first words of the message of La Salette. And at the end, the Virgin invites the two children to "make it known to all my people." With these gracious and reassuring words, Mary echoes nearly word for word the message given to the shepherds of Bethlehem on Christmas night: "Do not be afraid; for behold, I proclaim to you good news of great joy that will be for all the people" (Luke 2:10b).

Is it presumptuous to establish a parallel between the message of Christmas and that of La Salette? No, because in both cases Mary desires to give us the Savior. "For today in the city of David a savior has been born for you who is Messiah and Lord," (Luke 2:11), the angels announce, and the shepherds in a spirit of submission, go to see "this thing ... which the Lord has made known to us." (Luke 2:15b). At La Salette Mary presents Christ on her heart, the crucified Savior, inviting us to submit our lives to him. In both cases the spiritual attitude being proposed is the same: "Do not be afraid."

As we shall see, this basic invitation is addressed to women and men whenever God comes to meet them. We need only turn to Sacred Scripture.

## Throughout the Bible

"You need not be afraid of the people of that land," Joshua and Caleb told the Israelites in the desert of Kadesh (Numbers 14:9) as they were tempted to return to the tranquility of slavery in Egypt, rather than confront the risks of freedom. "Have no dread or fear of them," Moses insisted; "in the wilderness ... you saw how the Lord, your God, carried you, as a man carries his child" (Deuteronomy 1:29b,31a).

Several centuries later the prophet Jeremiah was told by God: " ... Prepare yourself; stand up and tell them all that command you. Do not be terrified on account of them" (Jeremiah 1:17). His vocation as a prophet began when he put all fear away, even though this would in no way shield him from insults and threats on his life.

We could mention a number of Old Testament figures who lived in the time of the Judges: Samson, Jephthah, Gideon, and later the young shepherd David confronting Goliath (1 Samuel 17:32-37). And then there are the prophets: Nathan condemning David for the murder of Uriah the Hittite in order to steal his wife (2 Samuel 12); Elijah demanding an account from the royal couple Ahab and Jezebel for the blood of Naboth, whom they slew to get his vineyard (1 Kings 2:19 ff.); Amos, Hosea, Isaiah, Micah—all courageous heralds of the word of God. Time and again God expects and inspires this beautiful spiritual attitude: "Do not be afraid!"

More radically, this invitation is one that Jesus uses throughout his public life most notably when he shows himself to his disciples on Easter morning. "Do not be afraid" (Matthew 28:5). "Do not be amazed" (Mark 16:6b). "Why are you troubled?" (Luke 24:38). "It is I. Do not be afraid" (John 6:20). "Peace be with you" (John 20:19,21,26b). Henceforth, the presence of the Risen One enables us to go beyond all fears and every anguish which arises in all the dramas of life. The refusal to yield to fear is a basic and definitive Christian spiritual attitude.

## In the History of the Church

But it is very far from being the case that this conviction of the Old and New Testament has become customary in the Church. The theologian, Maurice Bellet (1923-2018), has written a book with the significant title, *Fear or Faith*. And we have Jean Delumeau (1923-) to thank for *The History of Fear in the West*. Fear is the opposite of faith, as Jesus admonishes us in the Gospel: "Why are you terrified? Do you not yet have faith?" (Mark 4:40b) And how can we forget Karol Wojtyla's first words to the world on becoming Pope, October 16, 1978: "Do not be afraid! Open wide your doors to Christ the Redeemer!"

## Discovering a Loving Presence

Thus, Mary's invitation, *"Do not be afraid,"* at the beginning of her message expresses something essential to her people. The baptized are men and women called to conquer all fear. It is not a question here of a mere training of the will, still less of some kind of autosuggestion using the (Emile) Coué (1857-1926) Method ("Every day in every way I am getting better and better"). It is a matter of discovering, as did Maximin and Melanie, a loving and reassuring presence close to us.

Emile Coué (1857-1926), introduced a popular method of psychotherapy

At first, when they saw the globe of fire in the hollow of the gully, the children were frightened. Maximin tried

50

to reassure the girl. "Melanie, keep your stick and I will keep mine and if it does anything to us I'll give it a good whack!" But this very understandable fear disappeared completely when they heard her gentle and maternal voice. "It was like music", they would later say. They then huddled very close to her, and their only regret, after her departure, was that she had not taken them with her. Her presence was utterly peaceful. All their fear evaporated, by the gracious favor of the Beautiful Lady.

## Testifying in Our World

What causes all fear to disappear is discovering in our midst the presence of Jesus Christ our Savior, the Word made flesh, manifested to the shepherds at Bethlehem, crucified at Golgotha and risen on Easter Sunday morning. If the Christian no longer fears, it is because of the discovery, through faith, of the presence in this world of the God who saves. Our world urgently needs baptized people who bear witness to this faith which has no more fear.

The Statue of Liberty, symbol of America's welcome of immigrants

Fear not, when people try to frighten you with the insecurity of the suburbs or the "invasion" of immigrants. Don't be afraid to create bonds of active brotherhood and sisterhood. Don't be afraid, come what may, to work towards the economic development of poor countries and the rehumanizing of rich countries.

Fear not, you baptized, when people try to alarm you over the shortage of priests or the abandonment of religious practice. Don't be afraid to be believers sharing your faith, making the church present, however inadequately, as a sign of the presence of the Savior of Easter and of Christmas.

Let us recall, in conclusion, that Mary does not ask anything of us that she has not herself experienced. There is nothing wrong with feeling overwhelmed by the events of life, as she was from the Annunciation to the Cross, wondering each time what was happening to her. "Do not be afraid, Mary" she was told (Luke 1:30), and she gave her consent to the One for whom nothing is impossible (Luke 1:37-38). And so it was that Elizabeth could say to her, "Blessed are you who believed" (Lk 1:45).

At La Salette, Mary invites us to joy and not to fear.

# -6-
# My People

In her message Mary is eager to reach all her people. Three times she speaks of her "people": at the very outset, *"If my people will not submit ...",* and twice, at the end, when she invites the children to make her great news known to all her people.

Over one hundred years before the Second Vatican Council, she invites us to rediscover this reality which is an essential feature of biblical revelation-that God does not come to people as individuals. The divine plan is to save us collectively, through our membership in a people. It is within the People of God that we must live out our call.

## God's Plan

Beginning with the book of Genesis, God made this clear to Abraham, the father of all believers: "I will make of you a great nation ... All the families of the earth will find blessing in you." (Genesis 12:2b,3a). This plan for humanity, the establishment of a people peculiarly God's own, set apart from the start, was the very object of the divine promise.

That people, which belongs to human history, would take centuries to discover its vocation. When, after a long period of waiting, Isaac was born, and when, later, his son Jacob-Israel descended to Egypt with his twelve sons to escape famine, they were still a very small people, hardly conscious of being chosen by God. It would take the experience of the end of oppression and the departure from Egypt to make them realize little by little how totally they depended on God, their liberator and savior.

The Bible rightly speaks of a people formed like an infant in its mother's womb. The Virgin Mary, at La Salette, underlines this essential aspect of dependence on God when she says: *"If my people will not submit."* This dependence is sealed in the blood of sacrifice (Exodus 24:8) which binds God to this people and confers on them the vocation to live in a unique covenant relationship with God.

"For you are a people holy to the Lord, your God; the Lord, your God, has chosen you from all peoples on the face of the earth to be a people specially his own" (Deuteronomy 7:6 and 14:2).

"They are your people and your heritage" (Deuteronomy 9:29a).

"Thus, says the Lord: Israel is my son, my first born" (Exodus 4:22b).

"When Israel was a child, I loved him, out of Egypt I called my son" (Hosea 11:1).

This people is also God's spouse (Hosea 2:21; Jeremiah 2:2b; Ezekiel 16:8).

"You shall be to me a kingdom of priests, a holy nation" (Exodus 19:6a).

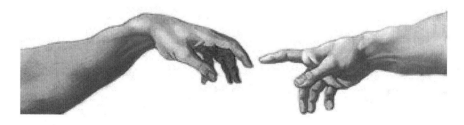

## Through Events

It was through the earthly events of its history that the Hebrew people became aware of being set apart, of belonging to God. They are members of Yahweh's family and live in intimacy with Him. They are destined to offer themselves, and the world, to God.

One would need to recall here all the events which forged this people: the nomadic life, oppression and deliverance, the wandering in the desert, the difficult acquisition of national unity, the divisions, the disastrous exile and eventual return. The people learned to read the signs of God through all these events. Happy events were received as gifts of God, unhappy events were calls to conversion.

The Virgin of La Salette takes her place in this grand vision when she speaks of the spoiled harvest and the famine as well as the superabundance of wheat. Slowly, painfully, through all these events, we have to become conscious of being the People of God.

# A New People

In the New Testament Jesus refines our vision of the People of God by rooting it in a new and definitive covenant. This people is an extension of that of the Old Testament. It was not by chance that Jesus chose twelve apostles. He wished thereby to mark the continuity with the twelve tribes of the old covenant. And, like the first, this new covenant will be sealed in blood, but this time with his own blood (Matthew 26:28).

As the Jewish Passover had been the precise moment of the birth of Israel as a people and the primary source of its life and unity, the Last Supper was the founding act of this new people. That is where Jesus gave it its specific character. Christ is now considered the new, the true paschal Lamb who dies for the whole world. And the true and definitive Passover is the meal during which he gives his flesh to eat and his blood to drink. The Lord's Supper is thus the source and origin of the new People of God, its permanent center, its bond of unity and its heart.

# By the Eucharist

The new People of God is the people born of the Body of Christ. Thus is realized in its fullness what the Old Testament had announced: "You will be my people and I will be your God" (see 2 Corinthians 6:16b Leviticus 26:12; Hebrews 8:10; Jeremiah 31:33; Revelation 21:3). This people is sanctified by the Blood of Jesus (Hebrews 13: 12). The sins of the people are wiped away by Jesus (Hebrews 2: 17). They are a

**Bread and wine for Eucharist**

people peculiarly God's own (Titus 2:14), a chosen race, a royal priest-hood, a holy nation (1 Peter 2:9). Thus Jesus brings into existence a new people which receives all the prerogatives of the old, but which surpasses it, rendering the old one void. And while the first people's horizon was limited to the earth, the homeland of the new People of God is in heaven (Philippians 3:20).

"All these died in faith. They did not receive what had been promised but saw it and greeted it from afar and acknowledged themselves to be strangers and aliens on earth" (Hebrews 11:13). Meanwhile, this people still sojourn here below, and its spiritual destiny which excels anything earthly is played out in temporal, historical and earthly events. This is the paradox of the Church: in the world, yet not of the world (John 17:14-16), it remains a visible people called to grow in time.

Our Lady of La Salette brings this truth to our attention in her own way by means of the incident of Coin which was decisive for Mr. Giraud. The spiritual destiny of each member of the People of God is at stake in apparently mundane events such as a poor harvest and a piece of bread given by a father to his child.

## A Universal People

This new People of God is not limited to any one people. It is open to all nations: "God first concerned himself with acquiring from among the Gentiles a people for his name" (Acts 15: 14). "Once you were 'no people' but now you are God's people" (1 Peter 2:10a see Romans 9:25-26).

And the Council made it clear that all people belong to the People of God in varying degrees of membership: Catholics, then the Orthodox, Anglicans, Lutherans, Jews, Muslims, all those who belong to other religions and finally all those who do not know God but strive to live good lives (*Lumen gentium*, 14,15,16).

## An Essential Belonging

In addressing her people, the Virgin of La Salette wishes to remind us of all the richness and all the demands of the vocation of humankind. Today still, through the happy or unhappy events of history, she invites us to recognize our belonging to the People of God, the people she wants to reach at all cost, as she shows by saying twice at the end of the message, *"Well, my children, make this known to all my people."* And she weeps because her people do not act as her people should. They reject God's plan. This is the people, born at the Last Supper, which no longer attends Mass, the source of its unity, or which does so only to make fun of religion.

The La Salette spirit must necessarily share Mary's concerns:

- *Service to all her people*, in society and common causes, while growing beyond our own individuality.

- *An understanding of our consecration.* The People of God is a people consecrated to God. This is essential.

- *An understanding of the Eucharist* as an assembly of the People of God, for that is what can unite men and women and form them into one people, thanks to the sacrifice of Christ.

"One soul alone have I to save," a once-popular hymn affirms. The issue of being open to all the dimensions of the People of God is as relevant as ever!

# -7-
# Submission

*"If my people will not submit ..."* But who is instinctively inclined to submit? Today's men and women are rightly wary of all forms of bondage. They jealously assert their freedom, especially where religion is concerned. Can we take seriously Mary's invitation in the opening words of her message? Here again, a rereading of the term as the Bible uses it will help us see how decisively Mary instructs us about our vocation.

Writing to the Christians at Corinth, St. Paul declares, "... everything belongs to you ... and you (are) Christ's, and Christ (is) God's" (1 Corinthians 3:21,23).

## All Things are Yours

Creation Window from the La Salette Parish,
Our Lady of the Cape Church, Brewster, MA, USA

Going back to the account of creation in the Book of Genesis, we learn that God has placed the whole world at the disposition of men and women. Created in God's image, Adam is called to subject all

59

animals to himself and to have dominion over the earth (Genesis 1:26-28). He will exercise his sovereignty over the universe by naming all things (Genesis 2:19). In these few words we see the immensity of the task the Creator has assigned. Men and women, masters of this immense universe, from the most distant galaxies to the realm of the infinitesimal; men and women, fragile as a breath, to them has the Creator confided the Creator's own task of subjecting all things.

Even more so than when it was written, can we marvel along with the author of the psalm: "When I see your heavens, the work of your fingers, the moon and stars you set in place—What is man that you are mindful of him, and a son of man that you care for him? Yet you have made little less than a god, crowned him with glory and honor. You have given him rule over the works on your hands, put all things at his feet" (Psalm 8:4-7). And we conclude with the psalmist: "O Lord, our Lord, how awesome is your name through all the earth!" (Psalm 8: 10). In other words, the glory of God is realized when humans subject the universe to themselves.

But it is also in our power to subject creation to vanity. In which case as Paul so clearly attests: "... for creation was made subject to futility, not of its own accord but because of the one who subjected it ..." (Romans 8:20). He restates, in his own way, what Chapter 3 of Genesis had affirmed: by refusing to submit to the Creator, humanity has dragged the universe down to destruction and death. Mary echoes this perspective: *"If the harvest is spoiled, it is all on your account"*, and evokes the image of the great famine and the death of little children.

The Second Vatican Council recalls this fundamental conviction. By refusing to recognize God as Creator, humans have by that very fact destroyed all harmony within themselves, with others and with all creation (*Gaudium et spes*, 13:1).

## You Are Christ's

If Mary wept at La Salette it is because she knows that this tragic human situation can be remedied. She wants us to open our eyes to the path which will enable us to succeed. Indeed, all of this world's realities will be humanized as they find their meaning in Jesus Christ.

Paul writes: "... everything belongs to you".., but he adds immediately, "and you (belong) to Christ, and, Christ to God" (1 Corinthians 3:21,23). When Mary uses the expression "to submit", she immerses us in the very essence of New Testament revelation.

Let us listen to Paul's famous passage to the Corinthians on the subject of the Resurrection (1 Corinthians 15:28): "When everything is subjected to him, then the Son himself will [also] be subjected to the one who subjected all things to him, so that God may be all in all."

Fr. Teilhard de Chardin, S.J. (1881-1955), a French philosopher and theologian

Father Teilhard de Chardin drew a great measure of his inspiration from this vision of the risen Christ, the culmination of the history of the universe, from the original Big Bang to the appearance of humans, the ultimate stage in the evolution of the mineral world to the vegetable kingdom, then to the animal world and on up to the human race.

## Christ is God's

But is further evolution, beyond humanity, precluded? Yes, unless humanity is willing to *submit* to one who is "beautiful in every way" (Song of Songs 4:7), Jesus of Nazareth, by acknowledging in him the Word made flesh, the very Son of God (see John 1:14). Slowly, mysteriously, the risen Christ, because he was "lifted up from the earth," received the power to "draw everyone" to himself (John 12:32). The evangelist St. John, in his account of the Passion, presents Christ as the "grain of wheat" falling to earth and dying (John 12:24) that he might be raised in glory (see John 12:28). This relates to the grand vision Paul describes in his gospel of the Resurrection (1 Corinthians 15: 1 ff.). At the end of human history and of the history of our universe all realities material and spiritual will be recapitulated in Christ, will become Christ. According to the divine plan, all things must return to God through Christ. At the completion of this grand adventure, Jesus will hand over all things to his Father, and then at last, one might say, God himself will be complete. In Paul's words: "God will be all in all" (1 Corinthians 15:28).

## A Communion

From the very outset of her message, Mary calls our attention to this fundamental vision. She comes to impress on us the responsibility that is ours as the People of God: to enable everything in our universe to find divine meaning ultimately through submission to Jesus Christ. How could we fail to see how extremely important this conception of the universe is as Mary briefly alludes to it? It is striking to note that all too often, human beings are asphyxiated by meaningless lives. We need only recall the growing number of suicides, especially among young people.

Mary's message invites her people to rediscover its mission: that all things human find their meaning in the spiritual attraction of the Risen One.

## Perspectives Long Forgotten

Such a vision of things opens up unsuspected perspectives, the very ones which the Council assigned to Christians as their task in the Constitution, *Gaudium et spes*, on the Church in the Modem World. Speaking "to all of humanity ... the Council wished to share with everyone its view of the Church's presence in today's world " (*Gaudium et spes*, 2). "The human person deserves to be preserved; human society deserves to be renewed" (*Gaudium et spes*, 3).

This, precisely, is what Mary had in mind when she appeared at La Salette. Submitting all things to Christ makes it possible for *"stones and rocks"* to become *"heaps of wheat"* in the world. Otherwise, there will come a *"great famine,"* and *"little children will die,"* and we shall have *"none but yourselves to blame."*

Vatican Council II, membership gathers for a session; photo: Lothar Wolleh

Like the Council Fathers, Mary believes that "in her most benign Lord and Master can be found the key, the focal point and the goal of all human history ... Hence in the light of Christ, the image of the unseen God, the firstborn of every creature (see Colossians 1:15)," Mary likewise "wishes to speak to all men in order to illuminate the mystery of the human being and to cooperate in finding the solution to the outstanding problems of our time" (*Gaudium et spes*, 10).

## The Incarnate Word, Light for Our Humanity

In the remainder of this Constitution, *Gaudium et spes*, the Council develops this idea more fully. Part I dwells on the human being as a person, then as a member of the human community, and finally as an agent in this world. Each of three chapters concludes with a consideration of the mystery of Christ.

"The truth is that only in the mystery of the incarnate Word is the mystery of the human being illuminated ... Christ ... fully reveals us to ourselves and makes our supreme calling clear" (*Gaudium et spes*, 22).

"This communitarian character is developed and consummated in the work of Jesus Christ. For the very Word made flesh willed to share in the human fellowship" (*Gaudium et spes*, 32).

"God's Word ... taught us that the new command of love was the basic law of human perfection and hence of the world's transformation ... Appointed Lord by his resurrection and given plenary power in heaven and on earth, Christ is now at work in human hearts through the energy of his Spirit... He animates, purifies, and strengthens those noble longings by which the human family strives to make its life more human and to render the whole earth submissive to this goal... The earthly service of human beings" makes ready "the material of the celestial realm" (*Gaudium et spes*, 38).

## In Our Day-to-Day Problems

*Gaudium et spes* does not hesitate to use the expression "to render the whole earth submissive to this goal".

Part II of this key Council document examines some especially urgent problems. To help people perceive where this *submission* of all human affairs to Christ comes into play, it includes questions pertaining to marriage and the family and the transmission of life. There are also questions relative to culture, economic and social life, the body politic, and lastly the preservation of peace in the community of nations, with special attention to the problem of nuclear arms.

## Submitting All Things to Christ

We can imagine the immense effort of conversion to which Mary calls us when, before anything else in her message she challenges us to submission. Just as her Son Jesus Christ submitted his entire human life to his Father, she urges all her people to be converted and thus "journey toward the consummation of human history ...: 'To re-establish all things in Christ.'" He is "the goal of human history, the focal point of the longings of history and of civilization, the center of the human race, the joy of every heart, and the answer to all its yearnings" (*Gaudium et spes*, 45).

There are other New Testament passages where the notion of subjection, submission, is once again encountered ... "He put all things beneath his feet and gave him as head over all things to the church" (Ephesians 1:22); "He will change our lowly body to conform with his glorified body by the power that enables him also to bring all things into subjection to himself" (Philippians 3:21); "... 'you crowned him with glory and honor, subjecting all things under his feet.' In 'subjecting' all things [to him], he left nothing not 'subject to him.' Yet at present we do not see 'all things subject to him ...'" (Hebrews 2:7b-8); and "[Jesus] has gone into heaven and is at the right hand of God, with angels, authorities, and powers subject to him" (1 Peter 3:22). What better way then, to conclude this chapter, than by rereading the hymn to Christ in Paul's letter to the Philippians (2:6-11). It tells us about the marvelous destiny of the entire universe called to be taken up by the Lord Jesus, the One who gave the example of submission even unto death, for the love of his brothers and sisters and of his Father.

"... (Jesus,) though he was in the form of God, did not regard equality with God something to be grasped. Rather, he emptied himself, taking the form of a slave, coming in human likeness; and found human in appearance, he humbled himself, becoming obedient to death, even death on a cross. Because of this, God greatly exalted him and bestowed on him the name that is above every name, that at the name of Jesus every knee should bend, of those in heaven and on earth and under the earth, and every tongue confess that Jesus Christ is Lord, to the glory of God the Father" (Philippians 2:6-11).

# The Six Days and the Seventh

*God reposing on Sabbath day*: Illustration from the first Russian Bible

*"Six days have I given you to labor, the seventh I have kept for myself; and they will not give it to me. this is what makes the arm of my son so heavy."* Disregard of the seventh day is, along with contempt for her Son's name, one of the two basic manifestations of the refusal to "submit", Mary tells us.

Are we to return to the precept of Sunday Mass, binding "under pain of mortal sin"?

Are we to join the devout in deploring the general decline of religious practice? This would most certainly be a misinterpretation of Mary's words. She will indeed speak of Sunday Mass further on in her discourse, but at this point she draws our attention to the correlation between the six days' work and the rest on the seventh day, which is reserved to the Lord.

## Free or Slaves?

In alluding to human work and rest, Mary directs our minds to some fundamental realities. As early as 1846, at the dawn of the industrial age, it was true that in the mines or the first factories, men, women and children were subjected to inhuman work schedules: sixteen hours a day, seven days a week! It was during this period that Karl Marx wrote his *Communist Manifesto*.

Struggles by labor unions today to guarantee the Sunday rest regularly dominate the news. But at a more fundamental level, every person's right to work is today being challenged across the planet. Meanwhile, children continue to be exploited-as many as 200 million of them worldwide.

The martyrdom of Iqbal Masih, a young Pakistani Christian, on April 16, 1995, at the age of 19, highlights the problem vividly. According to the Paris daily, *La Croix,* **(6)** "his desperately poor parents sold him for 80 francs when he was four. Then for six years he was chained twelve hours each day to a loom in a rug factory for a daily 20-centimes salary." **(7)** He was murdered on Easter Sunday.

## In Sacred Scripture

These burning issues of 1846 and of today refer us to the abiding relevance of biblical teachings concerning the six days and the seventh. The references are very numerous, as can be seen by consulting a detailed concordance of the Bible. **(8)**

We will limit ourselves here to these texts:

"Remember the sabbath day—keep it holy. Six days you may labor and do all your work, but the seventh day is the sabbath of the Lord, your God. You shall do no work, either you, your son or daughter, your male or female slave, your work animal, or by the resident alien within your gates. For in six days the Lord made the heavens and the earth, the sea and all that is in them; but on the seventh day he rested. That is why the Lord has blessed the sabbath day and made it holy" (Exodus 20:8-11).

"Observe the sabbath day—keep it holy, as the Lord, your God, commanded you. Six days you may labor and do all your work; but the seventh day is the sabbath of the Lord, your God. You shall not do any work, either you, your son or your daughter, your male or female slave, your ox or donkey or any work animal, or the resident alien within your gates, so that your male and female slave may rest as you do. Remember that you too were once slaves in the land of Egypt, and the Lord, your God, brought you out from there with a strong hand and outstretched arm. That is why the Lord your God, has commanded you to observe the sabbath day." (Deuteronomy 5: 12-15).

## Creator in Partnership with God

It is easy enough to discern the different tonality of these two texts. In Exodus, work is perceived positively as human participation in God's creative activity. The seventh day is therefore given to us so that we may enter into God's rest and recognize that our work is a sharing in God's own work.

## Freed from Slavery

The situation is different in Deuteronomy. In Egypt God's people suffered the harsh experience of slave labor. Work in this context is perceived as an affliction: "By the sweat of your face shall you eat bread" (Genesis 3:19). This pessimistic outlook on work as slavery likewise finds its place in the Bible (Job 7: 1ff.) and it is the fate of every human being! In this second perspective, the seventh

*Job Mocked by his Wife*
**by French Baroque painter**
Georges de La Tour (1593 – 1652)

day recalls the liberation from Egyptian slavery. God no longer appears as the Creator but rather as the Liberator. Without the weekly celebration of the seventh day, the people would quickly forget that they had been set free and the six days would soon become an enslavement again.

The people of the Bible further broadened this pattern. Along with the correlation between the six days and the seventh, they established, every seven years, a sabbatical year, and even, after seven times seven years, the jubilee year. These years were marked by the emancipation of slaves (Exodus 21:2), the canceling of debts (Deuteronomy 15:1 ff.) and the practice of allowing the land to lie fallow and rest (Leviticus 25:1-8).

In the midst of civilizations founded on slavery, one can guess how dynamic a principle of social upheaval this introduced! And when Mary at La Salette reminds us of the rhythm of the six days and the seventh, she too speaks of very basic realities.

## Entering into the Joy of God

In view of what the Old and New Testaments tell us about the seventh day, we can go further still:

"... the seventh day is the sabbath of complete rest, sacred to the Lord ... So shall the Israelites observe the sabbath, keeping it throughout their generations as a perpetual covenant. Between me and the Israelites it is to be an everlasting sign ..." (Exodus 31: 15a,16-17a).

"If you call the sabbath a delight, and the Lord's holy day honorable, ... then you shall delight in the Lord" (Isaiah 58:13b-14a).

"Therefore, a sabbath rest still remains for the people of God. And whoever enters into God's rest, rest from his own works as God did from his. Therefore, let us strive to enter into that rest" (Hebrews 4:9-11a).

When we compare these biblical passages with Mary's words about the seventh day, we see a little more clearly what a wonderful gift of God the seventh day is. Beyond the heartlessness of the world, the harshness of a life of labor, the hopeless violence which divides and torments humanity, the seventh day lets us enter into the joy of God. It introduces us to the beauty of the world created by God. It imbues us with the Spirit of Jesus who comes to create this world anew and to restore its original beauty. We are destined for rest and delights.

Every seventh day the Church sings, "Christ will come again." The songs of praise in our liturgies are identical to those in chapters 4 and 5 of the Book of Revelation, which describe the rest and delights of the seventh day. Here we find the hymn of praise of the blessed in honor of God the Creator (Revelation 4: 11) and in honor of Jesus Christ, the Lamb of God, slain and victorious in behalf of all humanity (Revelation 5:9-13). Together these reflect the two faces of God associated with the seventh day: God the creator and God the Savior.

## Light on Our Labors

Hence the importance of the seventh day. As a pilgrim remarked, it allows us to lift up our heads, to remember who we are-beings destined for joy. A Jacques Brel song goes, "Beyond the ugliness unfolding before us, we must gaze at the beauty that is." The seventh day is given to us precisely so that we may not lose sight of the beauty of God's world.

The entire effort of the six work days is brightened by the beauty the seventh day shows forth. All the work we do to create a world united with God, all the travail and suffering we bear in union with Jesus Christ to recreate it, are rooted in this beauty

St. Francis of Assisi
receiving the stigmata

which is revealed to us in the repose of the seventh day.

At the thought of this, Francis of Assisi used to dance for joy, playing an imaginary violin with two pieces of wood. And Francis de Sales speaks of "the blessed spirits lost in a twofold admiration: one before the infinite beauty which they contemplate and the other before the abyss of infinite beauty which they have yet to discover." Saint Anselm in turn exclaims: "What joy for you, O human heart, poor heart, accustomed to suffering and crushed by misfortunes! God's infinite happiness will be a source of incomparable joy for everyone."

## The Seventh Day and Sunday

The vistas opened up by the seventh day in the Old Testament are further broadened in the New. Here we see the gradual shift from the sabbath to the first day of the week, the day of the Resurrection. This is the day when Christians gather to devote themselves to the Word of God and the breaking of bread, as the episode of Paul at Troas demonstrates (Acts 20:7-12); on this day the solidarity collection is taken up (1 Corinthians 16:2). It is the day on which the author of Revelation (1:10) experienced his inaugural vision. The first day of the week, the new seventh day, opens before us an unheard-of future. We are destined to rise with Christ and to draw our life, starting now, from that paschal life.

This being the case, we can understand why Mary at La Salette attaches such importance to the seventh day. By neglecting it, we make ever weightier the burden of despair which shackles us. We have been created in fact to be creators with God, to accept the liberating gift which is bestowed on us in Jesus Christ, and to pass on to everyone the joy and dynamism of a risen world. Yes, Mary really wants to get us back to basics.

# -9-
# The Name of My Son

A medieval manuscript depiction of
the contraction of the name of God
(three leaf-like yods, Hebrew letters)

*"Those who drive the carts cannot swear without bringing in the name of my Son. These are the two things that make the arm of my Son so heavy."*

## A Pertinent Expression

The disappearance of blasphemy and the return of people to Sunday rest and religious practice following the apparition surprised the priests of the region of Corps, La Mure and other neighboring localities. They took this as an evident sign of people's belief in the authenticity of the Apparition and, especially, of a new awareness of God's presence.

The reverse was also true. Blasphemy and the widespread neglect of weekly Mass were evidence of a practical atheism and the rejection of God in society at large. The Blessed Virgin, in her message, demonstrates a keen insight into the current spiritual situation of the people of that period, particularly in the region around La Salette. The French expression "to swear like a cart-driver," the exact equivalent of the English, "to swear like a trooper," shows how prevalent the practice was. In the 19th century the bishops and priests of France established many confraternities or leagues against blasphemy. Beyond the pertinence of Mary's words at the time of the Apparition, however, we can once again discover in Sacred Scripture the enormous implications of her words. What is at stake is nothing less than acceptance of God's gift of grace, given to us through Jesus Christ.

## Blasphemy

Blasphemy, in the Bible, is an insult hurled directly at God. It is the very opposite of adoration and praise. It is the ultimate sign of contempt for God, and hostility and bravado towards God. Accordingly, it was severely punished under the Old Testament-death by stoning. "... whoever utters the name of the Lord in a curse shall be put to death. The whole community shall stone that person; alien and native-born alike must be put to death for uttering the Lord's Name in a curse" (Leviticus 24:16), a sentence Muslim fundamentalists favor to this day.

But we must not suppose that only the Old Testament recognized the gravity of blasphemy. In the New Testament Jesus was accused of blasphemy for calling himself the Son of God; this is the reason he was condemned to death. "... the high priest asked him, 'Are you the Messiah, the son of the Blessed One?' Then Jesus answered, 'I am' ... At that the high priest tore his garments and said, 'What further need have we of witnesses? You have heard the blasphemy. What do you think?' They all condemned him as deserving to die" (Mark 14:61-62a,63-64). The ultimate reason why blasphemy is so grave is that it is a willful rejection of divine Revelation and of God's work of mercy in our regard. This will be easier to understand if we meditate on the eminent place of the divine Name in revelation.

# God's Name Revealed

Already the names given to persons are of great importance in the Bible because the name reveals one's role in the world, one's social potential. It signifies the whole person. Thus, by changing Abram's name to Abraham, and later Jacob's to Israel, God indicates the new personality conferred on them in virtue of their being chosen.

Moses, afraid to look upon God in the burning bush (1897) by Charles Foster

If it is important to give names to human beings and to things, how are we to name God? The biblical divinity is not an abstract philosophical idea but is rather the one who has a name and gives it to us so we can name, address and enter into relationship with God. This is a God who has surrendered to us and over whom human beings therefore have a certain power, as one of the most beautiful pages of the Book of Exodus shows us: "'But,' said Moses to God, 'if I go to the Israelites and say to them, '.'The God of your ancestors has sent me to you," and they ask me, 'What is his name?' what am I to tell them?' God replied to Moses, 'I am who am.' Then he added: 'This is what

74

you shall tell the Israelites: I AM sent me to you.' God spoke further to Moses, 'This is what you will say to the Israelites: The Lord, the God of your ancestors, the God of Abraham, the God of Isaac, the God of Jacob, has sent me to you. This is my name forever; this is my title for all generations'" (Exodus 3:13-15).

The Name revealed to Moses can be interpreted in several ways: "I am the One who am," "I am with you." Whatever the exact translation, that name has been disclosed to us and it would justify the existence of an entire people for centuries to come. Israel would be the people that calls upon the name of Yahweh. The Decalogue expressly forbids taking that Name in vain for Yahweh is so fully identified with his Name that even to speak of "the Name" is to speak of God. This is the Name which is loved, praised and revered in the psalms. In fact, God will save an unfaithful Israel for the sake of that Name.

## For the Sake of That Name

Ezekiel, speaking in the name of God, relates to us the history of Israel's infidelity. At every important stage of this history, Yahweh plans to pour out his anger on this people, but, for the sake of his Name, saves them instead.

"I acted for the sake of my name, that it should not be desecrated in the eyes of the nations among whom they were ... I led them out of the land of Egypt and brought them into the wilderness. Then I gave them my statutes ... I also gave them my sabbaths to be a sign between me and them, to show that it is I, the Lord, who makes them holy. But the house of Israel rebelled against me in the wilderness. They did not observe my statutes ... My sabbaths, too, they desecrated grievously. ... I acted for the sake of my name, so it would not be desecrated in the eyes of the nations in whose sight I had brought them out. ... And you shall know that I am the Lord when I deal with you thus, for the sake of my name, not according to your evil ways and wanton deeds, house of Israel—oracle of the Lord God" (Ezekiel 20: 9a,10-11a,12-13a,14,44).

We may note, in passing, how this Chapter 20 of the prophet Ezekiel synthesizes several elements of Mary's message: the people's rebellion against God; the abandonment of the seventh day, the sabbath; God's anger blazing up against a sinful people; and mercy perpetuated for the sake of the holy Name. Who could still doubt that Mary at La Salette encourages us to draw from the divine source of the Scriptures?

## The Name of the Father and the Son

While the Old Testament reveals to us all the grandeur of God's Name, Jesus in the New Testament comes to make known the Name of his Father. By presenting himself as Son, he reveals his Father's Name. It is that Name which most completely expresses God's very being. He tells us in effect: My Father is your Father; my God is your God (see Luke 11:2; Matthew 6:9). And Jesus prays that the Father will glorify his Name: "'Father, glorify your name.' Then a voice came from heaven, 'I have glorified it and will glorify it again'" (John 12:28). Jesus exhorts his disciples to pray as he does: "Father, hallowed be your Name." (Another translation reads, "Reveal yourself as God.")

*The Annunciation:* **Orazio Lomi Gentileschi (1563–1639)**

We have come to know the Name of the Father, which is God's Name, because we have first known the Name of Jesus. This name, given at the Annunciation, signifies both his person and his mission as savior of the human race. It is translated "God saves" (see Matthew 1:21).

It is only when his human life has been perfectly consummated that Jesus receives the Name that is "above every name" as Paul says in the hymn quoted in the letter to the Philippians (2:6-11). This new Name received by Jesus is not distinct from God's and shares in its mystery.

That is the Name "Lord," Kyrios, the Greek translation for the Hebrew name of God.

The name "Lord"—occurring 725 times in the New Testament—has become the most common (not to say commonplace) Name of Jesus. We must be careful, then, not to forget its depth of meaning. For the sake of Jesus' Name, the disciples were happy to suffer (Acts 5:41), and missionaries set out on their journeys. The apostles performed miracles in his Name Mark 16:17-18).

Christians are those who are baptized in the Name of the Lord (Acts 5:41), who call on his name (Acts 2:21) and so submit to his authority. They also gather in his Name (Matthew 18:20) to give thanks, and then so live that their actions will give glory to that Name. At La Salette, in the portion of the discourse concerning the Name of her Son, Mary's rebuke goes right to the heart of the mystery of salvation. In denouncing our contempt for the Name of her Son, she is denouncing our contempt for and rejection of God's mercy on our behalf.

## No Other Name

One of Peter's discourses in Acts sheds a clear light on the above and will serve as an apt conclusion for this chapter.

"Then Peter, filled with the Holy Spirit, answered them, 'Leaders of the people and elders: 'If we are being examined today about a good deed done to a cripple, namely, by what means he was saved, then all of you and all the people of Israel should know that it was in the name of Jesus Christ the Nazorean whom you crucified, whom God raised from the dead; in his name this man stands before you healed. He is "the stone rejected by you, the builders, which has become the cornerstone." There is no ... other Name under heaven given to the human race by which we are to be saved'" (Acts 4:8-11).

# -10-
# Potatoes and Wheat,
# Walnuts and Grapes

The Blessed Virgin talking about potatoes! Some thought the very idea ludicrous. Certain civil authorities, on the other hand, found it disturbing. What if the farmers took Mary literally: *"If you have wheat, it is no good to sow it"*? Such superficial reactions aside, we are left to face the questions raised by the decidedly down-to-earth character of the message of this "Peasant Virgin," to borrow Joseph Folliet's term.

## Looking at Everyday Life

"What is ingenious about the La Salette discourse," a pilgrim once remarked, "is that Mary comes to speak to us about everyday life." A Breton leader of the Catholic Committee against Famine and for Development (CCFD) bestowed the title of "Our Lady of Development" on the Virgin of La Salette. Why?

It is obvious that Mary spoke primarily to peasant farmers. Through them she intended to address "all her people," yet those who till the soil made up her primary audience. She speaks to them about their life: blighted wheat, ruined harvests, walnuts, grapes and potatoes.

"A famine is coming...potatoes and wheat... walnuts and grapes..."

*A famine is coming*, a window from the Mary Keane Chapel, Enfield, NH,

79

We have already noted how severely the agricultural crisis was affecting the region, France and Europe, at the time of the Apparition. Mary proved to be an accurate observer of these agricultural disasters.

Not only did she observe them, she expects that we in turn will examine them closely.

*"I gave you warning last year with the potato harvest, but you did not heed it."* She wants to overcome our blindness. We have lost sight of the most elementary realities, realities vital to our lives as human beings. Through her message Mary confronts us with the momentous challenges of modern life, and with the perils that burden the future of the human race. Her tears and her words tell us that she cannot bear the sight of a great famine, still less that of dying children, always the first to fall victim.

At a deeper level, she shows forth the true face of God: a God who is pained to see people suffer. We can never repeat too often that this insight marked the starting point of Maximin 's father's conversion. He discovered a God who had observed the anxiety he himself experienced to see the wheat crumble to dust in his hands; a God who shared the concern of a father having no bread to give his child. *"You pay no heed."*

We must go further. Mary hopes our eyes can be opened. But, as she says, *"You pay no heed."* Humanity's plight is that it cannot and will not see. It refuses to face reality. This refusal "to pay heed," to see, potentially holds all of tomorrow's calamities.

If Mary were to appear today, what concrete situation would she call to our attention? Ecology? Nuclear power? Genetics? The economy? No one can say. What is certain is that she would invite us once again to look at the realities of everyday life, for these constitute the raw material of our spiritual adventure, the place where we either accept God's presence or refuse to recognize it, the place where, in any case, our destiny is played out.

## Our Lady and Development

What must we do so that *"the stones and rocks will change into mounds of wheat and the potatoes will be self-sown in the fields"*? The answer of "Our Lady of Development" is very clear: *"If they are converted."* She directs our attention to the root of the evil, a root that is of a spiritual order. She sees a direct relationship between blighted wheat and the refusal to submit to Jesus Christ. This is not some magical connection. This issue is our responsibility. "It is all on your account." When God's name becomes meaningless to us, when the seventh day no longer gives meaning to the work we do on the other six days, then we risk gradually destroying the environment and no longer taking heed of the victims of famine, not even the children.

If you desire the development of the whole person and of all persons, do not think first of the financial or material assistance which rich peoples are duty-bound to provide to poor peoples. That is the wrong way of looking at the situation. This is not a question primarily of reaching for our wallets. More and more poor nations are rejecting that kind of development, because it tears them from their roots and comes across as a form of domination wealthy nations exercise.

## Spiritual Realism

Mary invites us to conversion, that is, to the rediscovery of God, the Father of us all, who gave the earth to us all. At issue here is not whether rich nations should export their materialism to poor peoples, but whether we can attain mutual enrichment through the sharing of respective material, cultural and spiritual riches. We in our corner of the world, and they in theirs, have to let ourselves be changed, one by the other, and thus help each other rediscover the same unique model of integral development: Jesus Christ, the Word made flesh, a man rooted in the realities of everyday life, "God from God, light from light." That is why the "Peasant Virgin" comes speaking of wheat but bearing on her heart the image of Jesus to whom she begs us to submit.

And so, in meditating on the message of Mary at La Salette we learn spiritual realism. Yes, the contemplation of God is essential, but it must occur at the heart of the realities of the everyday life our fellow human beings live. Like Mary, we will uncover there the painful signs of God's absence, along with the signs of conversion and of the presence of this God who is the source of boundless life. We must contemplate the "warning" she gave "last year", but then take steps to transform our hearts and our world. Thus, does she see us infected with the Good News.

## Not Keeping Human Life
## Separate from Christian Faith

The kingdom of God is not an abstract reality outside our day-to-day human history. Today, as in 1846, people's "social, economic, political and cultural liberation will come about at the heart of these realities of human existence." (John Paul II, *Redemptoris missio*, 17). Such a liberation forms an integral part of the Reign of God that Jesus came to inaugurate on earth. Luke articulates it precisely in Jesus' inaugural discourse in the Nazareth synagogue: "The Spirit of the Lord ... has anointed me ... to proclaim liberty to captives and recovery of sight to the blind, to set the oppressed free." (Luke 4:18). Jesus came to bring about a real transformation of human relationships, beginning with people's material and human needs: I was hungry, I was thirsty,

I was sick, I was in prison ... and you came to me (see Mt 25). Mary's message at La Salette impresses on us Jesus' own evangelical pattern: conversion and development are inseparable.

## With and In the Church

The more one reflects on the message the more one marvels at its flawless construction. "Her Son Jesus Christ, her people the Church, and the world transformed and renewed," are inseparable. The conversion for which she pleads would consist precisely in never separating *my Son, my people* and the *mounds of wheat.*

**My Son:** If we isolate him from the fundamental needs of human beings, we always run the risk of presenting Jesus Christ in abstract and vague terms. Jesus Christ cannot be perceived here on earth without a community deriving life from him and bearing witness to him.

**My People:** The Church exists not to be closed in on itself, but to tum towards Jesus Christ and be the consummate servant of humanity.

**The mounds of wheat:** Development is of necessity, material, but remains illusory unless it is communitarian, that is, oriented to the service of the whole human community, taking Jesus Christ as its supreme model (John Paul II, *Redemptoris missio,* #59).

In the Church of today and tomorrow, the "Peasant Virgin" has much to teach us about the fulfillment of our mission.

# 11

# The Little Children Will Die

"Dragana, don't be afraid, they're only going to put a bandage on." This evening on television there are, yet again, unbearable pictures from Bosnia, and in particular that of a little child, Dragana, with her shattered leg.

I can never think of such things without remembering the hostile reaction of two young pilgrims, on their first visit to La Salette, when they first heard these words of Mary: *"Before the famine comes, the little children under seven years of age will be seized with trembling and will die in the arms of the persons holding them."*

What is so hard to take: Mary's message or, rather, our blindness in the face of the death of little children in the arms of their help-less mothers? This prophecy was fulfilled in and well beyond Corps during the years following the Apparition. Official records testify to an exceptionally high mortality rate among children. Mary condemns our indifference as adults. *"It is all on your account."* Children always pay the price of our personal and collective lack of responsibility.

## New Slaves

I will never forget the sight of all the babies who died of malnutri-tion at the hospital where I was stationed during the Algerian War of Independence. And can we forget the Palestinian children during the Intifada, or the Jewish children exterminated in concentration camps, or the children killed by the police in Brazil, and all the others who die every day in the Third World? In a radio interview, a fisherman in Brittany expressed his bitterness at not being paid for his work. But he was especially angry at those who import fish at low prices from countries where children are freely exploited, and not even paid. It was exactly the same in 1846 when, in France, the first coal mines were opened and children under the age of ten were put to work from ten to twelve hours a day.

The International Catholic Children's Bureau (ICCB) has published the charter of children's rights promulgated by the U.N. It regularly alerts the public to the thousand and one ways those rights are trampled in every part of the world.

## A Wake-Up Call from Innocent Children

*The cry of Rachel,* a fresco from Markov Monastery near Skopje, Macedonia

How could Mary at La Salette fail to alert us to the death of children? She knows only too well, through her experience on Calvary, what it means to hold one's dead child in one's arms. Today, as in King

Herod's day, she continues to weep over all those innocent children who are killed. "Come, all you who pass by the way, pay attention and see: Is there is any pain like my pain" (Lamentations 1:12a). "In Ramah is heard the sound of sobbing, bitter weeping! Rachel mourns for her children, she refuses to be consoled for her children—they are no more!" (Jeremiah 31:15; Matthew 2:18).

One Christmas night in Bethlehem, Father Schnydrig, a Swiss La Salette Missionary, was getting ready to celebrate Mass when he noticed a baby dying in the arms of its mother. There was nothing she could do. Fr. Ernst Schnydrig stayed with her and her husband. A few years later, he himself died just three days before the opening of the "Caritas Baby Hospital" for the care of preterm babies, which he had built thanks to the financial aid of both the Swiss and German Caritas organizations.

Fr. Ernst Schnydrig, M.S.
(1912-1978)

In Palestinian refugee camps, children receive the assistance which makes it possible for them to live, thanks to sponsorships organized by the Franco-Palestinian Medical Association. Thank God, many non-governmental organizations make it possible to thus save children threatened with death. The work of UNICEF is well known, but there is also the Catholic Committee against Famine and for Development, encouraging us to change present unjust structures in our own corner of the world and wherever children are dying in the Third World.

Like Mary at La Salette, will we learn no longer to tolerate the deaths of little children? Will the tears she shed over her Son on Good Friday, and the tears she sheds over the death of little children today awaken in us a sense of responsibility? **(8)**

# 12

# If They are Converted

Our Lady speaking with
Maximin and Melanie as the
workers in the fields below
gather their harvest

*"If they are converted, the stones and rocks
will be changed into mounds of wheat,
and the potatoes will be self-sown in the
fields."* After all that she has enabled us
to discover about the mystery of God
and of humanity, Our Lady now invites
us to draw the conclusion. *"If they are
converted ... ,"* she says.

This message of conversion is the
very one we find in the Bible, from
the prophets to John the Baptist. The
message was taken up by Jesus and
announced to the world by the apostles. It is the message proclaimed by the
Church down through the centuries.
And it is likewise the message proclaimed by the Second Vatican Coun-
cil. The famous word, *aggiornamento*, which John XXIII popularized
referred, it is true, to an updating of the Church as an institution.
But no reform is possible without conversion. Conversion applies not
only to pagans who become Christians; it is the work of a lifetime.
Once again, let us skim through the Bible.

## "Where Are You?"

In the Old Testament, the first warning God gave to the man and the
woman he had created in his own image was destined to deter them
from a desire to travel all the roads open to them-the basic temptation to move in every direction in order to learn, through personal
experience, what is good and what is evil. True liberty consists, on

the contrary, in *choosing the path that leads to life*, hence in choosing the one who knows that path, in other words, God. "The Lord is my shepherd ... He guides me along the right paths," as we sing in the 23rd Psalm (1a,3a). Sin is the opposite attitude: to think we are moving forward when, in fact, we are turning away from the one who is the source of life and liberty.

Salvation history is the history of God's Word addressed to men and women calling them to conversion and the right path by making them aware that they have lost their way. The first words of God to sinful humanity—"Where are you?" (Genesis 3:9b)—is a question inviting them to take stock of their true situation. But they are afraid. They are ashamed. Because they are naked now and have lost the garment of grace, of God's favor (see Saint Paul on "putting on" Christ, Romans 13:14).

## A Twofold Conversion

To regain this garment of grace, sinners must be converted. What does this mean?

"If they are converted... rocks will be changed into mounts of wheat..."

*If they are converted,* window from the Mary Keane Chapel, Enfield, NH

88

1. *They must turn back*, relinquish the choice they have made, make a new choice in the direction indicated by God. That is conversion of the heart.

2. This change of direction is accompanied by *moving in a new direction*. That is conversion in one's behavior.

These two changes or conversions, of the heart and of behavior, are linked together, but Scripture teaches us that conversion of the heart comes first. Without it, the modification in our behavior does not conform with what God requires. It would amount only to a surface change, masking the absence of a thoroughgoing change. We are always in danger of falling into the pharisaism against which Jesus contended so vigorously. Change of conduct is always secondary to conversion of the heart, just as, in the history of Israel, the Covenant always preceded the observance of the Law.

# A Believing Heart

The Covenant is the bond which unites God with the chosen people and that choice is gratuitous. The law is not a condition of the Covenant but a consequence of it. And what is asked of Israel, before all else, is *faith in the covenant* through the acceptance of God's gift. What must belong to God is first of all the heart, the center of one's personality, the profound source of one's free choices, the principle shaping one's attitude towards God and other people.

The prophets reproached the people of Israel precisely for their failure to believe in this God. Isaiah speaks in this vein to King Hezekiah who, frightened by the Syrian threat, no longer trusts in the Covenant: "By waiting and by calm you shall be saved, in quiet and in trust your strength lies. But this you did not will" (Isaiah 30:15b). Jeremiah's reproach is similar: "I warned your ancestors unceasingly from the day I brought them up out of the land of Egypt even to this day: obey my voice. But they did not listen or obey. They each everyone walked in the hardness of an evil heart in the stubbornness of their evil hearts ..." (Jeremiah 11:7-8a).

True confidence, true conversion of heart, is therefore the attitude of the person who awaits salvation from God alone. But the tragedy is that the human heart is evil, and we are powerless to change. Jeremiah insists that we are as incapable of conversion as we are of changing the color of our skin (Jeremiah 13:23).

Well, then, are we doomed to despair? No, of course not. On the contrary, we are driven to the true hope which expects everything from God. This is the meaning of Jeremiah's beautiful prayer: "Bring me back, let me come back, for you are the Lord, my God" (Jeremiah 31: 18b).

And how will God deliver us? By giving us a new heart.

"See, days are coming ... when I will make a new covenant with the house of Israel... It will not be like the covenant I made with their ancestors the day I took them by the hand to lead them forth from the land of Egypt. They broke my covenant, though I was their master ... But this is the covenant which I will make with the house of Israel after those days ... I will place my law within them and write it upon their hearts; I will be their God, and they shall be my people. They will no longer teach their friends and relatives, 'Know the Lord!' Everyone, from the leas to greatest, shall know me, from least to greatest, shall know me ... for I will forgive their iniquity and no longer remember their sin" (Jeremiah 31:31-34).

## Open to Christ on the Cross

What purpose, then, does the Law serve?

It is good in itself, but chiefly because it helps us discover from experience that we are unable to carry it out. It prepares us to renounce our claim to be God's equal and to open ourselves to the action of the Savior, which alone can bring about conversion of the heart and change of conduct.

*The Crucifixion* by Diego Rodríguez de Silva y Velázquez (1599-1660) Derivative work

"I will put my spirit within you so that you walk in my statutes" (Ezekiel 36:27a). This promise is fulfilled in the New Testament. In the Old Testament, conversion seems to be the work of God alone. But the Gospel tells us how this work is accomplished in the incarnate God. Salvation is consummated through Christ's act of love as he gives his life on the Cross. It is the Cross which, gratuitously, transforms us into children of God.

How does Christ transform our hearts? Through faith and conversion: "Repent, and believe in the gospel" (Mark 1:15). We must believe in the man Jesus, believe that God speaks through him and has made him the messenger of the Kingdom. Since all this is far from self-evident, a complete shift of perspective is required. It is foolishness, a stumbling block, says St. Paul, to believe that the reign of the living God is established through a human being, worse still through a crucified human being.

This belief requires a radical reappraisal of our idea of God and of our understanding of God's action in the world. Faith in the Cross is the sole means by which Jesus saves us. The Cross is the light of God's incredible love, the source of the heart's conversion.

Conversion of the heart is, therefore, belief in the Cross of Christ. But this conversion necessarily presupposes a change of behavior. The gratuitous love of Christ, which saves us by freeing us from sin, is a demanding love, calling us to be witnesses to his salvation and instruments of conversion for all our brothers and sisters. And here also, in this second phase—this "turning again" to God—we are asked to take on a radically new outlook on reality.

## Open to Our Brothers and Sisters

We need a spiritual compass to avoid deviating from the path where faith in Christ crucified has placed us. That compass is found in Chapter 25 of Matthew in the account of the last judgment: "Amen I say to you, whatever you did for one of the least brothers of mine, you did it to me ... Amen I say to you, what you did not do for one of these least ones, you did not do it for me" (Matthew 25:40,45). The road to follow, that radically new outlook on reality, is that of love for our brothers and sisters. Their limitations and faults make it difficult to love them, but Christ asks us to look upon them in a new way. Through them you reach me, he says. Hence to reach Jesus today we need to look at all those with whom we come in contact.

Finally, the conversion which the Gospel requires of us, that necessary conversion of which Mary reminds us at La Salette, will consist in our becoming children of God. To become a child of God is the conversion of heart. To remain a child of God is the conversion of behavior. "Unless you turn and become like children, you will not enter the kingdom of heaven" (Matthew 18:3).

# -13-
# Do You Say Your Prayers Well?

"Do you say your prayers well, my children?"

Window from the Mary Keane Chapel, Enfield, NH

"Is there anyone here who prays?" I put this question regularly to those Christians who come together for baptismal preparation. Generally, there is an embarrassed silence. Then a few timid hands go up. This shows how pertinent and timely was the question Mary asked in her message: *Do you say your prayers well, my children?*

To invite my listeners to reflect a little further, I then ask a second question: "Is there anyone here that never prays and has never prayed?" There follows another silence-this time of relief. Finally, one or two hands go up, but seldom more. Here, too, Maximin and Melanie's reply remains very timely: "Not very well, Madam!"

When Mary raises the question of prayer, she invites us to focus on a topic that is seldom discussed but which, nevertheless, is part of the lives of most people. The fact is that very few people have never turned to "that something or that someone above us", as it was once

93

put to me by an agnostic who would soon die of cancer.

## In an Agnostic World

Our western, secularized world has become largely agnostic. It no longer speaks about God, but about science, technology, economic growth. It is neither for nor against God. It simply has no need of God in its scientific research or its technical accomplishments.

Mary did not come to challenge this phenomenon but to invite us to realize that this world is not self-contained and that it is incapable of shedding light on life's ultimate meaning. She does not turn us away from our tasks as citizens of this world. Quite the contrary, she points out to us that God comes to meet us in all our "farms of Coin." She underlines our responsibility to provide heaps of wheat and potatoes. She comes to tell us that we fail at our task if we forget the basics. As St. Augustine put it, "You made us for yourself, O Lord, and our hearts are restless until they rest in you." That is why she questions us about our prayer.

> "Prayer is that moment when we acknowledge that God is our God, that God saves us, and that we are God's children ... Our mission in this world requires a bonding with the Lord who sends us, and hence there are moments when this bond seeks expression for its own sake."

This quotation comes from the 1973 meeting of the French Bishops' Conference in a document entitled A Celebrating, Praying Church. Already in 1968 they had asked:

> "What has become of prayer among the baptized who are now the priestly body of Christ for the world? What has become of prayer among those who correctly insist on Christians' commitment to humanity? It is certainly the hallmark task of Christians to lead the world towards its center of gravity—that of filial adoration" (Jesus Christ, savior and hope of people today).

This precisely is Mary's concern in her message at La Salette.

Prayer is, in our lives, that place of gift where our sense of God will be triggered. An incident in my own life greatly helped me to understand the gratuitousness and at the same time the value of prayer. It was during the Algerian war of independence. During a military operation we were passing through a mountain village. In front of us were a group of starving youngsters standing barefoot in the mud and icy rain. A fellow soldier who was an atheist and member of the communist party jeered, "Hey, priest! I suppose you'll solve all this by praying!" I long remembered that friendly provocation, without knowing how to answer. And I felt that uneasiness experienced by many Christians, even by religious, who ask themselves, "What good is prayer?"

## Why Pray?

"Not everyone who says to me, 'Lord, Lord,' will enter the kingdom of heaven, but only the one who does the will of my Father in heaven" (Matthew 7:21). We must be doers. But then prayer fades out of the picture, first for lack of time, then gradually out of a sense of futility. We see but two alternatives: atheistic rejection of prayer, or regression to a demeaning and false religiosity. That kind of misbelief is widespread and is challenged precisely by Mary when she asks, *"Do you say your prayers well, my children?"*

What we need to do, then, is to get beyond this misbelief by focusing on the specific role of prayer in the life of a believer. Prayer does not have the magic power to give us a hold on God so we can get what we want. On the contrary, I pray precisely because I know from faith that God "is at work until now" (John 5:17) to give life to humanity. I pray precisely in order to accept the gift of God who alone gives life. I pray precisely in order to enter into God's dynamism so that I may in turn act to give life to my brothers and sisters. And finally, I pray precisely to give thanks to God. This prayer of thanksgiving, joined to that of the Church in its liturgy, somehow makes God real in this world. How could God exist in this secularized world without the believers' prayer of faith? Let us now consider these three dimensions of prayer.

## Receiving the God Who Brings Me Into Being

First, we must feed on God's Word as found in Sacred Scripture in order to discover that the Word of God "enlightens everyone" (John 1:9) and that the Holy Spirit prompts our spirit to bear witness that we are God's children (see Romans 8: 16). Mary, in her message, does not speak of Sacred Scripture reading, but the biblical savor of her discourse strongly suggests it. Regular contact with Sacred Scripture is essential to awaken our very deepest desire, that is, of being acknowledged by God and of acknowledging God and finding pleasure in life with God. "One thing I ask of the Lord; this I seek: "To dwell in the Lord's house all the days of my life, To gaze on the Lord's beauty ... 'Come,' says my heart, 'seek [God's] face'" (Psalm 27:4,8).

We must immediately add, however, that this search is undertaken in darkness. According to Paul, prayer always involves a struggle. To the Colossians he writes of "Epaphras sends you greetings; he is one of you, a slave of Christ [Jesus], always striving for you in his prayers ..." (Colossians 4:12a). "I urge you, [brothers], by our Lord Jesus Christ and by the love of the Spirit, to join me in the struggle by your prayers ... that I may be delivered from the disobedient in Judea" (Romans 15:30-31a).

Abraham (Genesis 18:23-32), Jacob (Genesis 32:25-29) and Moses (Exodus 32:11-14) also experienced the harsh *struggle of prayer*. All prayer is ultimately the prayer of the poor and we will constantly need to entreat the Lord, "Teach us to pray" (Luke 11:1).

# Entering into God's Dynamism so as to Act

*The Prophet Micah* **by Hubert van Eyck (1366-1426)**

What I have gratuitously received from God I now extend to others in the struggle of everyday life by the practice of justice, goodness and humility: "You have been told, O mortal, what is good, and what the Lord requires of you: Only to do justice and to love goodness, and to walk humbly with your God" (Micah 6:8).

Prayer, in this second dimension, inspires me to give life to others, to all those whose needs cry out to me in the situations where life has placed me. The words of the prophet Micah admirably sum up the requirements of this second phase: the struggle to achieve justice and right for all people; all the richness that goodness brings to our relationships as brothers and sisters; and the walking in humility with my God. To pray, then, means being creative through my human activity. It also means letting God be God.

## Making God Real Through Thanksgiving

In this third dimension, we share in the joy of Jesus:

> "At that very moment he rejoiced [in] the holy Spirit and said, 'I give you praise, Father, Lord of heaven and earth, for although you have hidden these things from the wise and the learned you have revealed them to the childlike ... No one knows ... who the Father is except the Son and anyone to

whom the Son wishes to reveal him'" (Luke 10:21,22b).

God's gift of grace, which I accept and extend to others through my human actions, I now give back to God in joyful thanksgiving. Then God is fully acknowledged as God. The person who prays, in a certain sense, makes God real. Even if in the second phase of prayer, in the midst of human action, we encountered God's absence, prayer nonetheless gives thanks. And this thanksgiving will spring forth even when one is betrayed, when one is abandoned to the worst adversities, and when the world itself seems to have fallen victim to the worst horrors.

This is not spiritual masochism. Rather, like Jesus, it is a matter of giving thanks always, up to and including the moment of death: "Father, I thank you for hearing me. I know that you always hear me" (John 11:41-42). Prayer obtains God's favor, even in times of distress, and the love of the one praying can inspire others to look upon God with a similar love. Thus, the person who prays bears witness that God really deserves to be sought after because God's glory is humanity fully alive.

The episode of "the farm at Coin" and its epilogue, the conversion of Maximin's father, show us the extent to which prayer is essentially the entry into the dynamism of life which comes from God alone. After his conversion, Mr. Giraud entered every day into the prayer of thanksgiving which is the Eucharist.

## Evening and Morning

Learning how to pray and when to pray is no simple matter. At La Salette, Mary went beyond exhorting us to pray and determined both the rhythm and content of our prayer. *"Ah! My children, you must be sure to say them well, morning and evening, even if you say only an Our Father and a Hail Mary; but when you have time and can do better, you should say more."*

Mary is the one who, along with Joseph, taught Jesus himself to pray. She knows that there are particularly busy times in every human life: the life of the mother of a family, a very active professional life, or the demands of scholastic and extracurricular activities of children and adolescents. So she proposes a bare minimum. A lesser amount of prayer and the odds are we would lose our sense of the presence of God, Christ and the Spirit. She recommends in particular that we structure our lives around morning and evening prayer.

Christ praying in the garden of Gethsemane from the Methodist Church in Darlington MD.

The apostles, in the Gospel, were deeply moved at seeing Jesus devoting himself to prayer early in the morning or late in the evening, even though the crowds pressed upon him and his disciples to the point that they no longer had time to eat (Mark 3:20). "Rising very early before dawn, he left and went off to a deserted place, where he prayed" (Mark 1:35). "... he went up on the mountain by himself to pray. When it was evening, he was there alone" (Matthew 14:23).

Thus, Mary is simply exhorting us to imitate this morning and evening prayer of Jesus. Already the Old Testament was familiar with this rhythm of self-immersion at the very heart of God's presence: the evening and morning of the six days of creation when God saw that it was good (Genesis 1). The cloud, evening and morning, punctuated the desert wanderings of God's people (Numbers 9:15). The oil lamp (Leviticus 24:3) and later on, the morning and evening sacrifices in the temple (2 Kings 16:15).

Today as well, even in the midst of very active lives, men and women find that same minimal need to refresh themselves spiritually. This is why, for example, Catholic Action and other movements offer cassettes to help people pray the Scriptures while driving to work. Other pocket-size publications provide Scripture texts from the Mass of the day or excerpts from the Liturgy of the Hours.

# An Our Father and a Hail Mary

Mary also proposes a content for our prayer. First of all, she suggests the Our Father, the essential Christian prayer, taught by Jesus himself to his disciples when they expressed the desire to learn how to pray. When they pray this prayer, God's absence being duly acknowledged and accepted, believers welcome, at the core of their liberty, the mysterious presence of the Father who draws them. They pray first for the corning of God's Kingdom but do not separate it from daily bread or from the struggle against evil. This is at the heart of Mary's message that does not separate the mounds of wheat to be harvested from the People's submission to Jesus Christ.

Mary then adds the Hail Mary. By doing so she encourages us to live in her company. With her, the first of believers, we will discover God's presence ("the Lord is with you") every moment of our daily lives, from morning to night. We ask her to intercede in the two major moments of our lives-"now and at the hour of our death".

# Pray More, Pray Constantly

Beyond the bare minimum of an Our Father and a Hail Mary recited each morning and evening, Mary tells us, "When you have time ... you should pray more". A little earlier in her message she presented herself to us as one *compelled to pray ... without ceasing.*

Once again, she faithfully echoes the message of the New Testament. Luke (18:1) relates Christ's parable of the evil judge and the widow to teach us the importance of *praying always.*

The Acts of the Apostles (10:2) speak to us about the Roman official Cornelius who practiced almsgiving and *prayed constantly.* Paul gives the same exhortation (1 Thessalonians 5:17) but more often he speaks of his own *continual prayer,* for example, that he be given the opportunity to visit the Christians in Rome and to share his faith with them (Romans 1:10 ff.). He asks the Christians at Ephesus (Ephesians 6: 18) *to pray at every opportunity* for all the members of God's people.

He writes that he himself *does not cease praying* for the Colossians (1:9) that they may grow in the knowledge of God. Upon learning of the Thessalonians 's progress in the faith, he gives thanks to God and *prays unceasingly* (1 Thessalonians 1:2; 2 Thessalonians 1:3) that God may find them worthy of their calling. He likewise makes continued mention of Philemon in his prayers, giving thanks for his faith and love (Philemon 4). Each time there is insistence on a prayer that is unceasing and constant.

Two questions may be raised with regard to this invitation extended by the Virgin and the New Testament. Is it realistic? What can possibly be the reason for constant prayer? As for its being realistic, we need only think of monks and nuns since Mary's request certainly finds resonance among them. But is this appeal not also addressed to all her people?

Indeed, it is cause for deep joy to discover people who actually pray without ceasing. I recall a lady who lived in a new district of a large city. In the apartment complex where she lived, she met many people, natives and immigrants, who had left their world behind. All her encounters with them were permeated by her constant prayer. A famous priest, a friend of mine, visited her. He expressed his admiration. He had met many, many people in his travels as a speaker, but what had impressed him most was meeting this woman who prayed *more*. When she died, priests, the bishop, atheists, Muslims, the apathetic and the fervent alike, all made the same remark: "This woman was always praying."

## Dazzled by God

What is the reason behind such incessant and continuous prayer? Madeleine Delbrel (1904–1964) provides an answer.

"I was dazzled and remain dazzled by God. God becomes supremely important to us, more important than anything, than any life. Without this extreme, dazzling primacy of a living God, faith cannot endure. The true life of faith thrives in an atheistic environment. This bedazzlement, to be totally genuine, must be totally obscure." She calls this the black light. In a note on prayer she writes: "Without prayer, we cannot encounter the Living One, the One who speaks, the One who beckons, the One we follow." And a little further on she speaks of "those lightning flashes of prayer" which intensified in her "the need to go to the source; these occurred with increasing frequency, so vital and necessary was the source" (Madeleine Delbrel: Nous autres gens des rues, pgs. 286-287, Livre de Vie, Seuil, 1971).

## The Church of the Future

At the beginning of this chapter we asked, "Is there anyone here who prays?" Has prayer become an outmoded custom? Dietrich Bonhoeffer, our modem day prophet, makes the same point the prophetic teaching of Our Lady of La Salette does. From his prison cell he wrote of his vision of the Church of the future:

> "Our being Christian today will be limited to two things: prayer and righteous action for the human race. The word of God will be a new language, perhaps quite nonreligious, but liberating and redeeming as was Jesus' language ... It will be the language of a new righteousness and truth, proclaiming God's reconciliation with humanity and the coming of God's kingdom. Till then the Christian cause will be a silent and hidden affair, but there will be those who pray, and do right and wait for God's own time. May you be found among them!"

So he wrote to his godson on the occasion of his baptism. (Mary Bosanquet, *The Life and Death of Dietrich Bonhoeffer*, 1968, p. 259).

# -14-
# Going to Mass only to Mock Religion

In the first part of her message, Mary alerted us to the importance of the seventh day but did not mention the Eucharist. So, she returns to the subject in the second part, inviting us to recognize the seventh day as the day of Eucharist. While she laments the abandonment of the Mass by the majority of her people, she deplores perhaps even more a Eucharistic celebration that has become meaningless for those who participate in it, for those who seek to survive the boredom of winter by going to Mass but only to ridicule it.

The likelihood of people attending Sunday Mass as a distraction is hardly a threat today, but would not the routine of our religious practice and the reception of holy communion without appropriate reflection in themselves amount to a form of "making fun of religion?"

Mary's complaint at La Salette is indeed a call to examine our Eucharistic practice as God's people. Could we explain to our young people or to an unbeliever what the Mass means to us? We will try here to review briefly the essentials of the Eucharistic mystery.

# The Eucharist: An Assembly

Let us try to imagine for a minute that Mass is no longer celebrated anywhere in the world. How would the Church remain visible? Some, of course, would see no problem in this. But in this scenario, we ask how Jesus Christ would be known? The Eucharist therefore is not a private devotion; it is inherently a gathering. On the evening of Emmaus, it was essential that the community come together once more, for only through the community would the Risen One manifest himself and prepare his future witnesses. This first aspect has serious consequences. "We should not stay away from our assembly" (Heb 10:25), for by so doing we deprive the Body of Christ of our presence. The issue here is the visibility of Jesus Christ in our secularized world where, in truth, there is no longer any other visible sign of God's presence.

This coming together is not blind to our conflicts. It is a gathering of sinner-saints on the road to reconciliation. It is up to us to find the way to express this when we gather. The assembly subsists in its ordained ministers, priests, who alone are the signs of its true identity. It is not a private club; it is one with the whole Church throughout space and time. It is the responsibility of all, in union with the bishop, to call and prepare the ordained ministers which the Church absolutely cannot do without. (10) Sunday services in the absence of priests can only be provisional. If this situation were to continue, the very Eucharistic structure of the Church would be jeopardized.

# The Assembly: Where the Word is Received

The first act of the assembly is to receive the Word of God whether in a passage from the Old Testament, a psalm, the writings of the apostles or the Gospel. The Virgin's language at La Salette moves us to discover how this Word is actualized in our own history. Treated like a museum piece, the Word would be of no interest. As Jesus declared in the synagogue at Nazareth (Lk 4:21), what matters is what the Word means today. Would not failure, on the part of the People of God, to take seriously the hearing and the proclamation of the living Word, be in-itself a very grievous *"making fun of religion"*?

# Assembled to Give Thanks

How could we fail to thank the Father when he gathers us together around his Son whose Word reveals his saving action? "Let us give thanks to the Lord our God." This is the heart of the Eucharistic Prayer, and the Church takes up in its own name the prayer of Jesus at the Last Supper (Luke 22:17,19).

"He gives thanks to his Father at the very hour when he prepares himself to carry out his yes as a Son in the yes of the Cross". **(11)** The Church joins in this thanksgiving of Jesus; in his "thanks". In fact, etymologically, Eucharist means thanks.

We can also "make fun of religion", therefore, by failing to cultivate a proper Eucharistic attitude, that is, by not making of our entire lives a thanksgiving to God for all the beautiful things he is accomplishing in our brothers and sisters and in ourselves. Little by little, such an attitude pulls us out of the production-consumerism cycle into the spirit of the gift outright, this in a world marred still by violence and deceit.

# To Save From Oblivion

Bishop Oscar Arnulfo
Romero in 1978

Although we are immersed in that kind of world, Christians do not lose heart because in sharing the bread and wine we make *remembrance* of the Body given up for us and the blood poured out for us. Like the disciples at Emmaus, assembled Christians celebrate the memory of Holy Thursday, Good Friday and Easter. They remember the evening of the Last Supper, with both its tragedy and infinite tenderness, when Jesus washed their feet and shared with them the bread and wine, his Body truly given up and his blood truly shed on Good Friday. And above all they relive that moment beyond time when Christ arose from the tomb. Sometimes the Church relives this memorial with unexpected realism, as in the case of Archbishop Oscar Romero (1917-1980), who was assassinated at Mass, while reading the gospel of the grain of wheat that dies (John 12).

Mary at La Salette insists we drink from this inexhaustible source of love. So do the bishops:

> "When the time for the Last Supper had arrived, Jesus knew what awaited him: the fury of his enemies and his judges, the cruelty of his executioners, the treason and abandonment of his disciples, his own solitude. Nevertheless, by his actions at the Last Supper, he gave a radically new meaning to the confrontation which was to reach its climax on Calvary. In the midst of people's rejection of God, he goes on living in the presence of his Father, commending his life into the Father's hands and loving his own to the end. By thus carrying love and fidelity to the extreme, he makes his death the starting point of a new existence not only for himself but for his disciples to whom he gives his body and blood. By this gesture carried out once and for all, he opens before us the path to a life in keeping with his own." **(12)**

Mary at La Salette exhorts us to "submit" our lives to the Eucharistic Presence, the one force capable of leading us on the road to total conversion, the road of reconciliation and liberation. She shows us, crucified on her breast, the One who has conquered hatred. She especially wants us to be nourished by him so that we will have the courage to preach reconciliation to a humanity that at first sight seems beyond reconciliation. If we refuse to labor at bringing about such a liberation, this would be yet another way of making a mockery of religion.

# Invoking the Holy Spirit on the bread and the cup, and on the assembly

Too often Christians in the West forget the Holy Spirit who is nonetheless the one who comes to irradiate on our human world the entire liberating energy of the Eucharist. Our Western Church needs to turn towards the Holy Spirit and to emphasize the Spirit's presence in the Eucharistic liturgy. In the Mass there is a twofold Epiclesis or invocation of the Holy Spirit: the first on the bread and wine that they be transformed into the Body and Blood of Christ; the second on the people assembled that they become the Body of Christ in the world. The Holy Spirit alone can effect this twofold transformation that brings about the real presence of Jesus crucified and risen in our world.

Thanks to the Spirit, the assembly does not remain closed in and centered on itself but is propelled outward towards the Lord and towards the world. The assembly disperses so that the shadow of the Cross of the Risen One may establish in this world "a new heaven and a new earth" (Revelation 21:1a). Thanks to the Holy Spirit, the bread and wine "which earth has given, and human hands have made" are transformed into the body and blood of the Lord, thus anticipating the transformation of the world. Possessing "the power ... to bring all things into subjection to himself" (Philippians 3:21), Christ is the world's future. **(13)**

If Christians gathered for communion do not place themselves at the service of the Holy Spirit for the work of transforming the world and changing *"rocks and stones into heaps of wheat"*, is Mary not justified in saying, *"They go to Mass only to make fun of religion"*?

## Assembled to Receive Christ in Holy Communion

Accustomed as we are to receiving holy communion, we are no longer shocked, as were the Jews and as our uninitiated contemporaries likewise are, at the idea of eating the body and drinking the blood of Christ (John 6:60-61). And yet, when we assemble, it is not only to celebrate a memorial, but it is to receive communion as well. "Whoever eats my flesh and drinks my blood has eternal life, and I will raise him on the last day" (John 6:54 ). Jesus "eagerly desired to eat this Passover" with us (Luke 22:15).

So then how could Mary at La Salette not invite us to that weekly Eucharistic rendezvous? But in order that we might not make fun of religion, she proposes that we take to heart Paul's admonition to the Corinthians: "A person should examine himself, and so eat the bread and drink of the cup. For anyone who eats and drinks without discerning the body, eats and drinks judgment on himself" (1 Corinthians 11:28-29).

What does that mean? Of course, it does not mean returning to the mistaken practice of the past when people felt obliged to go to confession every time they received communion. What Paul is telling us in chapter 11 of his first letter to the Corinthians is entirely different. He is reproaching the Christians for engaging in an act of eucharistic communion without living in true communion with their brothers and sisters. "When you come together it is not for the better but for the worse. There are divisions among you, ... factions .... When you come together, it is not really to eat the Lord's supper .... Each of you goes ahead with your own supper, and one goes hungry while another gets drunk" (1 Corinthians 11:17-21).

The call of Our Lady of La Salette is therefore a catechumenal summons addressed to the whole Church. She wants to lead all Christians, old and new, to the Eucharistic table because there would otherwise be no Church. But she also wants Christians to discern the Body of the Lord so that we might truly become the Body of Christ, offering ourselves and our lives, in union with our brothers and sisters, for the service of humanity.

## Assembled to Share in Christ's Mission

There is only one Church. The Eucharistic Church is inseparable from the missionary Church. "Go in the peace of Christ", we are told at the end of Mass. The whole assembly of the baptized is sent forth.

We are sent forth that we might be in this world the people bearing the face of the suffering Just One, "without whom no village, no city nor, indeed, our whole world, can endure" (Aleksandr Solzhenitsyn, 1918-2008). This people will bear witness to the triumph of faith and to the truth which makes us free. We will be a people of sentinels, alert to all the signs of hope human life offers, a people of brothers and sisters living in solidarity and mutual sharing. The practice of the Eucharist gradually grows into the practice of the Beatitudes.

## Conclusion

We are called, then, to become a people of 'martyrs' who find in Christ crucified and glorified the strength to witness, to struggle, and even to love our enemies and pray for them. In this world with its sometimes unbreathable atmosphere of deceit, violence and mediocrity, it may well be that 'martyrdom,' lived collectively throughout life and made fruitful by the Eucharist, is the only really effective means of showing that nothing "will be able to separate us from the love of God in Christ Jesus our Lord" (Romans 8:39).

These concluding lines are from the document entitled Bread Broken for a New World. We make them ours as we end this meditation on the words Mary spoke concerning the 'mystery of faith.' But we would need a lifetime to be fully assimilated to the Eucharist in all its richness and to realize how truly it is "the fount and apex of the whole Christian life" (Vatican II, *Lumen gentium*, 11).

# -15-
# During Lent They go to the Meat Market Like Dogs

*"During Lent they go to meat market like dogs..."*

Window from the Mary Keane Chapel, Enfield, NH, USA

Mary's comment about Lent is rather harsh and the comparison with dogs, we must admit, gags us.

But the Bible's references to our faithful companion are likewise unflattering: "As dogs return to their vomit, so fools repeat their folly" (Proverbs 26:11). The second letter of Peter (2:22) applies this proverb to the false teachers who poisoned the life of the primitive church.

The final chapter of the Book of Revelation calls for the expulsion from the Christian community of "dogs, sorcerers, the unchaste, murderers, idol-worshipers, and all who love and practice falsehood" (Revelation 22:15). Who these dogs are, we are not told, but it would not be surprising if the expression referred once more to false teachers. Targeted for persecution by underhanded Judaizing teachers,

Paul warns the Christians of Philippi: "Beware of the dogs!" (Philippians 3:2).

A surprising instance of this comparison with dogs is found on the lips of Jesus. It occurs at his meeting with the Syrophoenician woman (Matthew 15:26). He calls the pagans dogs, much as the Jews did in his time. But this gentle Lebanese woman will not allow herself to be put off. She responds in kind thus anticipating the opening of the Gospel to the Gentiles.

False teachers, pagans-these are the object of the comparison with dogs. In taking up that expression, Mary at La Salette suggests that the conduct of the People of God during Lent is that of pagans. Mentioning this after speaking about prayer and the Mass, she clearly wishes to draw our attention to something essential to the life of her People.

## Putting our Vocation as Christians to the Test

Lent recalls the time Jesus spent in the desert. Immediately after his baptism, on the threshold of his public life, he was led into solitude by the Holy Spirit and spent a symbolic (but very real) period of forty days during which he was tried by temptation as were his people of old when they set out from Egypt. He faced the trial of hunger. He was tested by the absence of God, just as at Massah and Meribah when the people demanded to know, "Is the Lord in our midst or not?" (Exodus 17:7). Satan says to Jesus in the desert, "If you are the Son of God" (Matthew 4:3). At La Salette Mary comes to remind her People that they need this desert experience and must, in the footsteps of her Son, put their Christian vocation to the test.

## The Ascent Towards Easter

The temptation of Jesus in the desert remains an unfinished episode. Luke (4: 13) makes clear that his Passion and Cross will be Jesus' supreme temptation. Each year the Christian observance of Lent prepares us to celebrate the paschal mystery, going through the suffering of the Cross with Christ in order to rise with him.

The Council stresses the importance of this privileged season especially for the Christian initiation of catechumens. The church thus disposes them also to enter into the paschal mystery through the reception of Baptism (*Decree on the Missionary Activity of the Church, Ad gentes,* 14). The document on the Liturgy, *Constitution on the Sacred Liturgy, Sacrosanctum concilium, (109)*, singles out the penitential character of Lent, a preparation, as ever, for the celebration of the paschal mystery.

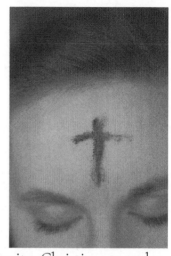

Each year on Ash Wednesday, the Gospel invites Christians to undertake a threefold program of discreet prayer, fasting and almsgiving.

Since the Council, the church in many countries highlights the continuing relevance of Lent by giving fasting, almsgiving and prayer a collective dimension through participation in such Lenten campaigns as the Catholic Campaign against Famine and for Development (CCFD), Catholic Relief Services (Operation Rice Bowl), Oxford Committee for Famine Relief (OXFAM), etc. These programs encourage the nascent realization that we must share with the poor of the world if we are to achieve development through solidarity.

We will not repeat here what was said earlier about "Our Lady of Development". We will, however, conclude this chapter by observing that the severe words she spoke with reference to Lent harmonize perfectly with what she says about" stones and rocks" becoming "mounds of wheat". The Lenten programs Catholic Relief Services and others sponsor are an excellent way of putting into action, concretely, the conversion Mary asks of us at La Salette.

# -16-
# To All My People

"You will make this known to all my people."

Window from the Mary Keane Chapel, Enfield, NH, USA

*"Well, my children, you will make this known to all my people. Very well, my children, be sure to make this known to all my people."*

**Marie des Brulais:** "What did you take the Blessed Virgin to mean when she told you to make it known to all her people?"
**Melanie:** "I understood that I was to tell it."

**Marie des Brulais:** "But what does the word 'people' mean? Do you think that the Blessed Virgin meant only the people in this region?"
**Melanie:** "I don't know. I understand it to mean everybody."

**Marie des Brulais:** "Ah, so you think it isn't just France?"
**Melanie:** "I don't know. I take it to mean everybody."

**Marie des Brulais:** "But if you were to be put to death for all this, would you be silent?"

**Melanie:** "Oh no! We would only die once, and once I was dead, I would never die again."

These were Melanie's replies on September 19, 1847, when she was interviewed by Marie des Brulais, the schoolteacher from Nantes who followed the activities of the two children between 1847 and 1855. As these answers show, they had understood the universality of the Beautiful Lady's message. And Melanie naively and quite spontaneously declared herself willing to give her life in support of her testimony.

Once again, we come upon the biblical and evangelical flavor of the La Salette message. The four gospels likewise end on a missionary note.

"Go, therefore, and make disciples of all nations," the risen Jesus told the eleven (Matthew 28:19). He had previously said to the women, "Go tell my brothers to go to Galilee, and there they will see me" (Matthew 28:10). Mark's gospel originally ended with the fear experienced by the women, who "said nothing to anyone, for they were afraid" (Mark 16:8), even though they had received the same instruction as in Matthew. In the conclusion that was later added to Mark's gospel, however, Jesus commands the eleven, "Go into the whole world and proclaim the gospel to every creature" (Mark

*The Disciples of Jesus baptize* by James Tissot (1836-1902); photo: Brooklyn Museum

16:15). In Luke, the Risen One says that "repentance, for the forgiveness of sins, would be preached ... to all the nations ... You are witnesses of these things" (Luke 24:47-49). John is no less definitive: "As the Father has sent me, so I send you" (John 20:21). This sending forth is rooted in the intimacy of trinitarian love. The mission is an over-flowing of that love in the direction of all humanity.

It is wise to weigh the contemporary import of Mary's words of sending-forth. In his encyclical, *Redemptoris missio*, of December 1990, John Paul II does not hesitate to affirm that the Church's missionary efforts are yet in their beginnings. Some believe this document will remain one of the most important of this pope's reign. Reflecting on it, one is readily struck by its consonance with the message of La Salette.

In his introduction he takes note of the fact that, since the Council, the number of people who do not know Christ has doubled. It remains nonetheless true that all are loved by the Father. Missionary commitment is always a sign of vitality in the Church. It should therefore be a passionate concern of all Christians. Rather, its decline is symptomatic of a faith crisis. One can understand, then, Mary's insistence at the close of her message. She not only says *"You will make this known"* but *"(Be sure to) make this known to all my people"*.

## To Announce Jesus Christ

This missionary urgency has to do with making Jesus Christ known. "But how can they call on him in whom they have not believed? And how can they believe in him of whom they have not heard? And how can they hear without someone to preach?" (Romans 10:14-15).

This injunction remains even more relevant in this day and age when inter-religion dialogue and development are seen as indispensable aspects of our mission. "The Church's mission is to direct the attention of humanity towards Christ... because all people are included in the mystery of redemption. Christ is the one savior of all, the sole media-tor through whom we enter into communion with God" (*Redemptoris missio*, 4,5). The newness of Jesus of Nazareth is freely offered to all people (*Redemptoris missio*, 7). Even to those people who will never know him or never even hear of him, salvation in Christ is accessible by virtue of a grace which comes from the Church, even if they do not belong to it. This gift which enlightens their lives is a grace which comes from Christ, is communicated to them through the Holy Spirit and enables them to cooperate in their own salvation (*Redemptoris missio*, 10).

Mary at La Salette bears on her heart the radiant image of Jesus crucified and risen, and she comes to tell us that no one can have any other final destiny than that of "submitting" to her Son.

This does not in any way diminish our profound respect for the religious beliefs or human convictions of others. Still, every human being needs Christ who alone has conquered sin and death. The mission thus gives us the opportunity to demonstrate our faith in Jesus and in his love for us. Paul tells us in his letter to the Ephesians that the Christian must not keep to himself "the inscrutable riches of Christ" (Ephesians 3:8).

## Working to Build the Kingdom

Jesus Christ came on earth to proclaim the Kingdom of God hidden in the heart of the world. To work on behalf of the Kingdom is to recognize and foster that divine dynamic which can transform human history. Mary does, in fact, call us to conversion that stones, and rocks may become heaps of wheat. She does not separate our acceptance of Jesus Christ from the task of transforming the earth so that it may serve the needs of all.

## In the Dynamism of the Holy Spirit

The Holy Spirit is the prime agent in the Church's mission. A reading of the Acts of the Apostles makes this abundantly clear. We see the

Spirit at work both in those who announce the Gospel and in those who accept it. The apostles have a different language for preaching the Gospel to the Jews, the pagans, the Greeks and the people of Asia Minor. Mary at La Salette was an attentive missionary too, when she spoke "otherwise", in the local dialect, to Maximin and Melanie, who did not understand French. She truly inculturated the Gospel in her message.

John Paul II tells us that in his travels he has been able to contemplate the varied action of the Holy Spirit in non-Christian cultures and religions. Mary could likewise see in Mr. Giraud, on the road back from the Coin farm, worried that he had no bread for his child, a father like those in the gospel to whom Jesus says, "If you then, who are wicked, know how to give good gifts to your children, how much more will the Father in heaven give the holy Spirit to those who ask him?" (Luke 11:13).

## The Urgency of Proclaiming God Today

The proclamation of Jesus Christ, the effort to build up the Kingdom, the dynamism of the Holy Spirit-these, according to John Paul II, are the three principal foundations of the mission. He goes on to indicate more precisely the new fields of missionary activity and the level of personal and ecclesial commitment the proclamation of the God of Jesus Christ to the whole world requires. Mary, at La Salette, reveals herself totally dedicated to that mission. She invites us to live by the Word of God and to be its heralds. "Live it! Speak it!" was the slogan adopted a few years ago by the national action campaign of the Young Christian Workers (YCW). Both are necessary. To speak the message without living it is utterly useless. Living according to the Gospel without ever speaking about it is inadequate. Proclamation is wanting.

It is imperative today that we proclaim Jesus Christ and the entire Good News. A young man dying of AIDS remarked one day to his mother, "Maybe you didn't speak enough to me about God." Mary at La Salette shows us an ailing world, threatened by death in so many ways and she knows it is in tremendous need of her great news. So, she can only say to us as did Jesus her Son, "Go on your way; behold, I am sending you ..." (Luke 10:3). Christ has suffered, he is risen; preach conversion in his name (see Luke 24:46-47). "Go, therefore, and make disciples of all nations" (Matthew 28:19). *(Be sure to) make this known to all my people.*

# To Pray, to Take Pains, to Suffer

**Mary shares her message with young Maximin and Melanie**

Challenging words that describe the difficult road which Mary says we must walk!

These three expressions used by Mary in her message indicate to us what she is compelled to do in the face of her people's refusal to submit their lives to Jesus Christ. They show how far she is willing to go to keep her people from being abandoned by her Son.

If the People of God have given the title of Reconciler of Sinners to the Virgin of La Salette, it is because they have fully understood Mary's trifold commitment to their service: *"I am compelled to pray to him without ceasing in your behalf; you will never recompense the pains I have taken for you; for how long a time do I suffer for you!"*

## I am Compelled to Pray Without Ceasing on Your Behalf

At the outset of the Apparition, Mary presents herself to us in a prayerful attitude, she is seated, her face is buried in her hands. She was a great woman of prayer throughout her life. In prayer:

- *she accepted* the Word of God at the Annunciation (Luke 1:38);

– *she shared* her exultant prayer of joy with her cousin Elizabeth (Luke 1:46);

– *she prayed* in anguish when Joseph considered dismissing her quietly (Matthew 1:19);

– *she prayed* as she joined in the awe of simple folk at Christmas (Luke 2:19);

– *she prayed* in terror at the massacre of the innocents (Matthew 2:18);

– *she prayed* in a spirit of dedication in the temple, with Joseph and her Son (Luke 2:27);

– *she prayed* as a Palestinian refugee in Egypt (Matthew 2: 14);

– *she prayed* at a time of anxious seeking (Luke 2:48);

– *she prayed* as a mother becoming a disciple as she discreetly came to the aid of young newlyweds (John 2:3);

– *she prayed* in a time of family interference (Mark 3:21); she prayed the blessed prayer of one who kept the Word throughout her lifetime (Lk 11:27-28);

– *she prayed* at the foot of the cross as she accepted her mission as mother (John 19:26)—a mission inaugurated on Pentecost in the cenacle with the apostles at prayer (Acts 1:14).

This mission continues after her Assumption and Vatican II speaks to us of her ongoing intercession (*Lumen gentium*, 62).

## The Pains I Have Taken for You

Mary tells us we will never be able to repay her for those pains. Her expression is important. She has not been content to pray; she has been active, she has taken pains.

She was actively at work in Nazareth. Every day she went to draw water at the town spring-an obscure, tiring and monotonous chore still familiar to millions of women in the Third World. Yes, Mary was no stranger to hard work.

Mary was active in the service of others: for Jesus and Joseph (thirty years), for the elderly Elizabeth (six months), and later for the newlyweds at Cana. Mary was active particularly by her willing assent to events. In his encyclical, *"Marialis cultus, For The Right Ordering And Development Of Devotion To The Blessed Virgin Mary"*, Pope Paul VI speaks of the woman who "gave her active and responsible consent ... to that 'event of world importance,' as the Incarnation of the Word has been rightly called" (#37). Mary can speak in all truth of the pains she takes in our behalf and those she will go on taking. More so than St. Therese of Lisieux, she is "spending her heaven doing good on earth".

## For How Long a Time Do I Suffer for You!

Besides praying and taking pains, Mary goes yet further. She suffers for us. It grieves her to see her Son's arm weighing heavily on us, revealing the tremendous weight of her people's resistance, the full extent of their obstinacy and the ravages that ensue. Like her Son at Jerusalem (Luke 19:41), Mary wept over this resistance.

Beyond these tears, there remains only the consent she gave to her Son's passion, for "No one has greater love than this, to lay down one's life ..." (John 15:13). "For Christ, while we were still helpless, yet died ... Indeed, only with difficulty does one die for a just person,

121

though perhaps for a good person one might even find courage to die. But God proves his love for us in that while we were still sinners Christ died for us" (Romans 5:6a,7-8).

In the very trying world that is ours today, can there be another approach to prayer other than the one Mary comes to teach us? Not only to pray, but to become involved ... to agree to stand with Jesus crucified. Not for the love of suffering, but like Mary at La Salette, out of impassioned love for Jesus Christ who came to give his life for the world (John 6:51).

# -18-

# The Virgin's Tears
# and Her Crucifix

"I saw her tears flow, how they flowed and flowed, and halfway to the ground, they melted into the light." Thus did Melanie describe Mary's tears at La Salette.

We can associate those tears with the crucifix which Mary bore on her heart. Instruments of the Passion—a hammer and pincers were placed near the arms of the Cross, symbolizing either our resistance or our conversion. The choice is ours.

Statue in La Salette
Community Chapel
on the Holy Mountain

Her complaint is easy to understand. How well we understand and hear her plea: *"For how long a time do I suffer for you ... you take no heed of it. However much you pray, however much you do, you will never recompense the pains I have taken for you!"*

## Jesus Weeps

The tears, the crucifix and these words of Our Lady are at the heart of the mystery of La Salette and bring us back to the heart of Christian revelation. Mary's tears recall those Jesus shed over Jerusalem.

"As he drew near, he saw the city and wept over it, saying, 'If this day you had only known what makes for peace—but now it is hidden from your eyes. For the days are coming upon you when your enemies will raise a palisade against you; they will encircle you and hem you in on all sides. They will smash you to the ground and your children within you, and they will not leave one stone upon another within you because you did not recognize the time of your visitation'" (Luke 19:41-44).

These are the tears of one who is powerless to keep those he loves from destroying themselves blindly. Jesus weeps because he has failed to convince them to stop resisting God's visitation. His tears plead with them one last time to open their eyes. They are one final effort to forestall and prevent the calamity which is to befall the heedless.

Jesus' tears are the next-to-last effort his love for humanity attempts. Blessed Angela of Foligno quotes Jesus as saying, "My love for you is no laughing matter."

## The Servant of God Offers Himself Out of Love

The last stage of this love will be that of offering his life. Resolutely, Jesus accepts the mission of the "suffering Servant" who takes upon himself the unhappiness born of people's blindness.

The well-known text of Second Isaiah will be quoted here in its entirety because it is fully consonant with what Mary reveals at La Salette about her commitment, at his side, to her Son's mission as redeemer.

*Isaiah*; artist:
Providence Lithograph Co.

We will follow the interpretation which recognizes in this text four successive interventions: God expresses astonishment, the pagan nations make a surprising discovery; the prophet becomes a suppliant; and the last word in confirming the success clearly announced from the outset rests with God. Let us reflect on Deutero-Isaiah:

**God Speaks (Isaiah 52:13-15):**

"See, my servant shall prosper, he shall be raised high and greatly exalted. Even as many were amazed at him—so marred were his features, beyond that of mortals, his appearance beyond that of human beings—So shall he startle many nations, kings shall stand speechless; For those who have not been told shall see, those who have not heard shall ponder it."

**The pagan nations discover that they have been redeemed by the Servant (Isaiah 53:1-6):**

'Who would believe what we have heard? To whom has the arm of the Lord been revealed? He grew up like a sapling before him, like a shoot from the parched earth; he had no majestic bearing to catch our eye, no beauty to draw us to him. He was spurned and avoided by men, a man of suffering, knowing pain, Like one from whom you turn your face, spurned, and we held him in no esteem.

"Yet it was our pain that he bore, our sufferings he endured. We thought of him as stricken, struck down by God and afflicted. But he was pierced for our sins, crushed for our iniquity. He bore the punishment that makes us whole, by his wounds we were healed. We had all gone astray like sheep, all following our own way; But the Lord laid upon him the guilt of us all."

**The prophet beseeches God on behalf of the suffering Servant (Isaiah 53:7-10):**

"Though harshly treated, he submitted and did not open his mouth; Like a lamb led to slaughter or a sheep silent before shearers, he did not open his mouth. Seized and condemned, he was taken away. Who would have thought any more of his destiny? For he was cut off from the land of the living, and smitten for the sins of his people. He was given a grave among the wicked, a burial place with evildoers, Though he had done no wrong nor was deceit found in his mouth.

"But it was the Lord's will to crush him with pain. By making his life as a reparation offering, he shall see his offspring, shall lengthen his days, and the Lord's shall be accomplished through him."

**God Responds to the Prophet's Prayer (Isaiah 53:11-12):**

"Because of his anguish he shall see the light; because of his knowledge he shall be content; My servant, the just one, shall justify the many, their iniquity he shall bear. Therefore, I will give him his portion among the many, and he shall divide the spoils with the mighty, Because he surrendered himself to death, and was counted among the transgressors, Bore the sins of many, and interceded for the transgressors."

Jesus no doubt meditated at length on this Suffering Servant poem, one of the high points of the Old Testament. For in it he discovered his true vocation, namely, to fulfill the mission of this perfect disciple of God.

The suffering Just One offers his love to God and God makes his suffering a sacrifice of expiation. His offering and intercession wrest humanity from its perversity, maladies and obstinate resistance.

"Upon him was the chastisement that makes us whole, by his stripes we were healed" (Isaiah 53:5). Love which offers its suffering will bear much fruit: "Because of his anguish ..., My servant, the just one, shall justify the many, their iniquity he shall bear" (Isaiah 53:11).

# Fighting Every Evil

Appearing at La Salette, Mary turns our attention to this mystery of the fruitfulness of love giving itself in the midst of suffering. It is not a question of enjoying suffering - every means must be taken to combat it. Jesus certainly was no lover of suffering. He saw it as something evil, the sign of that more radical evil, sin. Accordingly, he struggled with all his strength against whatever suffering he encountered. He comforted, cured, put people back on their feet, restored sight, hearing and speech.

We must fight against every kind of suffering and evil.

As we are well aware, however, the tragic element of human existence still will not go away. There will always be the young married woman who dies of cancer in a matter of weeks; the man who kills his mother and daughter, tries to kill his wife, and then commits suicide; the sudden death of a baby; death by torture or summary execution; or in a collective massacre.

Any commitment necessarily supposes sacrifices, and at times even unjust, undeserved suffering. Wherever love is offered, there will always be those who, incomprehensibly, reject it. Faced with that kind of suffering, one can, as many do, rebel and demand an accounting from God. But the fact remains that "For those who have not been told shall see, those who have not heard shall ponder it" (Isaiah 52:15).

Our Lady in tears, Our Lady bearing on her heart Jesus crucified, with the hammer and pincers, Our Lady of La Salette, invites us to unite ourselves to Jesus, the Suffering Servant. She also invites us to unite ourselves to her, the perfect disciple of her Son. *I am compelled to pray to him without ceasing ... The pains I have taken for you! For how long a time do I suffer for you!"*

In the presence of all who *"take no heed,"* including ourselves, she insists, *"However much you pray, however much you do, you will never recompense the pains I have taken for you."*

She is saying what St. Paul said, "Join with others in being imitators of me ... and observe those who thus conduct themselves according to the model you have in us. For many, as I have often told you and now tell you even in tears, conduct themselves as enemies of the cross of Christ. Their end is destruction" (Philippians 3:17-19a). And again she invites us to make our own the words of Paul, "... in my flesh I am filling up what is lacking in the afflictions of Christ on behalf of his body, that is, the church" (Colossians 1:24b).

## Entering into the Mystery of the Cross

Saint Paul is obviously aware that there is nothing lacking in the power of Christ's cross to save the world. But he allows himself to be seized by the Lord so as to be associated with his sufferings. The letter to the Hebrews takes up the subject again. "Remember the days past when, after you had been enlightened, you endured a great contest of suffering. At times you were publicly exposed to abuse and affliction; at other times you associated yourselves with those so treated" (Hebrews 10:32-33).

*Crucifixion* by Rembrandt (1606-1669); scanned by Szilas

He then recalls the trials of that long line of biblical believers. We too are invited to "persevere in running the race that lies before us while keeping our eyes fixed on Jesus, the leader and perfecter of faith. For the sake of the joy that was set before him he endured the cross, despising its shame, and has taken his seat at the right of the throne of God. Consider how he endured such opposition from sinners, in order that you may not grow weary or lose heart. In your struggle against sin you have not yet resisted to the point of shedding your blood" (Hebrews 12: 1b-4).

There is no doubt that this is the road along which Mary, by her tears and her crucifix, wishes to lead us at La Salette.

Countless men and women who have visited her on that mountain have felt themselves powerfully drawn into the mystery of the cross of Christ! Mary has inspired them to stand beside her at the feet of the Crucified One whom they have come to recognize in the features of all who suffer today.

## Tears of Light and a Resplendent Crucifix

We must recall that, in the final analysis, "Mary's tears melted into pearls of light and that her crucifix was the most brilliant part of the apparition." We need to recall also that, in the closing phases of the apparition, Mary rose from the ground and raised her eyes towards heaven. Only then did her tears cease to flow.

This was her way of telling us that we should look at humanity, tried by suffering, in the light of the Risen One. According to the letter to the Hebrews, Christ, after enduring his Passion, is forever seated at the right hand of God.

Just as Mary stopped weeping, one day all tears will be dried. The book of Revelation states this quite clearly.

"After this I had a vision of a great multitude, which no one could count... Then one of the elders spoke up and said to me, 'Who are the ones who have survived the time of great distress; they have washed their robes and made them white in the blood of the Lamb ... God will wipe away every tear from their eyes'" (Revelation 7:9a,13,14,17b).

The same book confirms this in the vision of the heavenly Jerusalem. "Then I saw a new heaven and a new earth ... 'Behold, God's dwelling is with the human race. He will dwell with them and they will be his people and God himself will always be with them [as their God]. He will wipe every tear from their eyes, and there shall be no more death or mourning, wailing or pain, [for] the old order has passed away.' The one who sat on the throne said, 'Behold, I make all things new.'" (Revelation 21:1a, 3-5a).

Chaplain Bill Devine from Boston, MA,
gives communion to Marine during Mass in the field

# A Message of Joy

After hearing the story of La Salette for the first time, two teenagers remarked, "What a downer! This is a message of doom—nothing but famine and dying children." A priest echoed their sentiments: "Have you ever seen the Blessed Virgin cry? Honestly, such nonsense!"

Some theologians voice these same reactions, wondering how Mary, now in heaven, can say to us, "For how long a time do I suffer for you." Is it not totally incongruous, therefore, to speak of joy at La Salette?

Joy, nonetheless, broke out at La Salette on that 19th of September 1846, as Maximin and Melanie testified. "Afterwards (after the Beautiful Lady had disappeared) we were very happy and went back to taking care of our cows." They experienced joy in this heavenly vision of Mary surrounded by light and garlands of roses. When Maximin was asked why he never married, he replied, "When you've seen such a beautiful lady, you don't care to look for another."

## Surprised by Love

Joy spread along with the news of the apparition. Of course, it also aroused unbelief, notably in the case of Maximin's father. When Pierre Selme announced in the local tavern on September 20, 1846, that the boy had seen the Blessed Virgin, Giraud was roundly ridi-

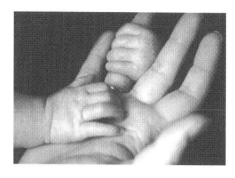

"Thus says the Lord: 'See, upon the palms of my hands I have engraved you'" (Isaiah 49:8a,16)

culed. He refused to listen to his son until that moment when Maximin mentioned the episode at the farm near Coin. Suddenly Mr. Giraud *realized that he was loved by God*, that God was concerned about him. In the life of any person, the discovery that "somebody loves me" is the source of the deepest possible joy. Its wonder fills every bride- or husband-to-be in the world. But their joy takes on an unexpected dimension when, beyond that, they realize that God takes an interest in their love.

How many pilgrims, following in Giraud's footsteps, have experienced the joy of being loved by God!

There was joy also for the priests when they witnessed the conversion of their parishioners. At Corps, at La Salette and throughout that region people were finding their way back to the Church and to a faith community.

There has also been joy among the sick who were cured after drinking water from the spring which had begun to flow at the feet of the weeping Mother. Yet how much greater is the joy accompanying the great number of spiritual cures known only to the many priests who, from 1846 to this day, have ministered to the pilgrims.

"Ah! if only the confessionals could speak," priests used to say. The confessionals have been removed but the reality of the Sacrament in reconciliation rooms remains a source of enduring joy.

And how could we fail to mention the joy and amazement of those who for the first time discover the extraordinary beauty of the locale of La Salette? Mary carefully chose the place where she came to visit her people. The majesty of the mountains, the variety of the flowers, the splendid sunsets all year round, the unique, surreal atmosphere of the sea of clouds—all speak of the Beautiful Lady and her homeland, heaven.

In spite of its "rough exterior," Mary's message itself is meant to lead us to joy.

*"Come near, my children, be not afraid! I am here to tell you great news."*

## A Road to Joy

The Basilica on the Holy Mountain in France, enveloped in a sea of clouds

From her first words the children were captivated, no longer frightened, much like the shepherds of Bethlehem on Christmas night. That Good News announced a great joy to all the people. This great joy is being offered to us, it cannot be imposed. It is up to us to choose it freely, to accept it. That is the reason why the Virgin's message is built around two conditional phrases: *"If my people will not submit... If they are converted."* True joy always demands a real commitment, both on the personal and communal levels.

Mary speaks about her people. The Bible tells us that humanity's joy lies in belonging to God. "I heard a loud voice from the throne saying, 'Behold, God's dwelling is with the human race ... they will be his people and God himself will always be with them [as their God]'" (Revelation 21:3); and the prophet Isaiah does not hesitate to say, "As a bridegroom rejoices in his bride so shall your God rejoice in you" (Isaiah 62:5b).

If Mary comes to speak to her people, she does so to invite them to walk this road to joy once again. This is the one road we are called to walk.

That is why she invites us to submit, not to become slaves, but "subjected" to Jesus Christ, "so that God may be all in all" (1 Corinthians 15:28). This saying of Paul is surprising, even staggering. It suggests that God is not completely God, so to speak, or that God's joy is not complete, until God is all in all.

## The Joy of Solidarity

What is said about the arm of her Son is no less stunning. It is not a question of an avenging arm. It is, rather, the same use of arm that we find in Isaiah: "Here comes with power the Lord God, who rules by his strong arm" (Isaiah 40:10a). If this arm were not heavy upon us, would we realize the extent to which we have weighed it down?

Would we realize that we have nailed that arm to a cross? If it weighs on us, it is not to crush us, but in order that, in the joy of forgiven sinners, we may discover that it is a saving arm.

*"For how long a time do I suffer for you!"* Mary openly reveals her suffering to us. That is a painful realization. But when we discover that someone has suffered for us, is not our heart filled with gratitude and joy?

To learn that we have not been abandoned, to discover that someone shares our suffering in a spirit of solidarity is a deep joy even in the midst of the worst trials.

Anyone who is active with Amnesty International or other nongovernmental organizations has heard this from the victims whose causes he has championed.

## Different Facets of Joy

I am thinking of a Jesuit priest working in Algeria amid the current upheavals. His young university students are amazed that he has remained with them to share their sufferings. Each year he returns to

La Salette to refresh his spirit at the feet of the Blessed Virgin.

When we are faced with the miseries of the world, we may be tempted to give up in despair. However, we can also see those who take pains, not because they enjoy suffering but because they want to take up the challenge of solidarity. And we can get ourselves involved, which will be a source of joy for us even if it means self-denial. Thus does Our Lady of La Salette wish us to walk the way of risk-taking.

Young Marcel Schlewer (back row, second from left)
and his Army buddies in Algeria

I am thinking of a Christian who was struck by the climate of despair within the media, but who admires the way a major Christian weekly regularly opens its columns to those who, in the most difficult situations, are struggling to carry on.

When the Blessed Virgin speaks of the seventh day, she is speaking of the day of joy *par excellence*. But in a time of high unemployment we come to perceive the *"six days to work"* also as a source of joy. A little further on Mary speaks of the Name of her Son. Those who accompany catechumens in their baptismal preparation are well aware of the joy they experience when they are able to call God by name!

We know well how a farmer takes pride in a good harvest. Very often, rural populations have a greater capacity to appreciate the ongoing wonder of the seasons and of harvests of grain and other crops. Mary comes to alert us to the risk we run of disturbing and even destroying God's gift of "abundant harvests" (Luke 10:2) and of "wine to gladden our hearts" (Psalm 104:15).

*"Ah! my children, you do not understand. Well, wait, I will say it differently."* And Mary repeated in the local dialect what she had just said in French about the harvest. It was a joy for her to make herself understood, especially by the lowly and the simple.

And later when she speaks to us of *"doing penance by the famine,"* the prospect is anything but cheerful. Nevertheless, if we reread the Gospel episode of the prodigal son, famine was the first and inevitable step leading to the explosion of joy at the father's extravagant welcome. "Quickly bring the finest robe and put it on him; put a ring on his finger and sandals on his feet. Take the fattened calf and slaughter it. Then let us celebrate with a feast, because this son of mine was dead, and has come to life again; he was lost, and has been found" (Luke 15:22-24).

## The Joy of Choosing Life

Pilgrims make their way in procession with prayer and song
on the Holy Mountain of La Salette

*"If they are converted, the stones and rocks will be changed into mounds of wheat."* Conversion, the return to God, is our deepest joy. It is expressed in the abundance of newfound life.

"Rejoice with me because I have found my lost sheep" (Luke 15:6b). "... there will be rejoicing among the angels of God over one sinner who repents" (Luke 15:10). The Father is supremely happy to be on good terms with his children: "My son, you are here with me always; everything I have is yours," the father said to his elder son (Luke 15:31b). And his joy is then to give lavishly.

Of course, God does not do for us things we can do for ourselves. Potatoes never grow on their own! But putting our shoulder to the task at hand and showing some imagination come easily to us once we realize how much God loves us.

The remainder of Mary's message shows us the different paths of conversion, or how we can achieve joy.

First, prayer. It is the place *par excellence* where joy will be found, for it is an encounter with the One who is Love. When we become aware that this prayerful contact with God transforms us, then our joy increases at the thought of sharing a new life with the One who loves us.

St. Paul insists on prayer as a source of joy in many of the letters he addressed to the various communities.

- To the Christians of Thessalonica he writes, "Rejoice always, Pray without ceasing" (1 Thessalonians 5:16-17);

- to the Philippians, "Rejoice in the Lord always. I shall say it again: rejoice! ... in everything, by prayer and petition, with thanksgiving" (Philippians 4:4,6);

- to the Colossians, " ... giving thanks to the Father, who has made you fit to share in the inheritance of the holy ones in light" (Colossians 1:12);

- to the Romans, "Rejoice in hope, endure in affliction, persevere in prayer" (Romans 12:12).

– And he expresses a wish for them: "May the God of hope fill you with all joy and peace in believing, so that you may abound in hope by the power of the holy Spirit" (Romans 15:13).

Peter, in turn, follows suit. He notes that:

– Christians "… rejoice, although now for a little while you may have to suffer through various trials" (1 Peter 1:6).

– "You rejoice with an indescribable and glorious joy" (1 Peter 1:8), for "the God and Father of our Lord Jesus Christ… in his great mercy gave us a new birth to a living hope through the resurrection of Jesus Christ from the dead" (1 Peter 1:3).

How could the Mass not be the pinnacle of joy? The word "eucharist" comes from a Greek verb meaning to render thanks for the unimaginable gift of the death and resurrection of Christ, a gift which is renewed for us in the bread which was multiplied when Jesus gave thanks for it (John 6:11; Matthew 15:36). Paul recalls that he received and has passed on the Lord's supper, at which Jesus gave thanks (1 Corinthians 11:23-24).

We cannot forget that Lent also is a sign of joy: the joy of sharing, the joy of the ascent towards Easter. Besides, doesn't Jesus in the Gospel urge us not to put on a Lenten face (Matthew 6:16-18)?

We recall, finally, the joy of the episode which occurred at the Coin farm. It sums up the message's entire call to joy. Of course, we must make this joyful message known to *all the people* (Luke 2:10). Then we will know the joy of being apostles, the joy of witnessing to Christ, the joy of giving "life … more abundantly" (John 10:10b).

## The Joy of the Cross

Mary's tears at La Salette express suffering and are not a symbol of joy. But they are reflective of the Gospel beatitudes, "Blessed are they who mourn, for they will be comforted" (Matthew 5:4).

The one who charted this paradoxical road towards happiness is the very one who was impatient to receive the baptism of the cross (Luke

12:50). Those thousands of people who suffered the savagery of the cross would have been surprised to learn that this instrument of torture would one day become a sign of joy and hope. The joy of the cross is by no means derived from suffering, but the discovery that in Jesus Christ it has become the sign of the greatest love.

When Jesus realized that his compatriots were obstinate in their refusal of the gift of God which he was offering, when he saw that his enduring love was met only with hate and violence, it was evident to him that this conflict would lead to nothing less than his passion and death.

Fr. Jerome Saw Eiphan, a La Salette Missionary from Myanmar, stands atop nearby Mount Gargas

But his horrible death on the cross would not be, first and foremost, the victory of the forces of evil. It would be before all else the total offering of his love to his Father through his love for his human brothers and sisters. "This is why the Father loves me, because I lay down my life in order to take it up again. No one takes it from me, but I lay it down on my own. I have power to lay it down, and power to take it up again. This command I have received from my Father" (John 10:17-18).

The command received from his Father is not a death sentence, but rather the order *to give (his) life.* As Jesus says in his discourse at the Last Supper, "No one has greater love than this, to lay down one's life for one's friends" (John 15:13). Saint Paul elaborates on the meaning of the cross of Christ in his letter to the Romans. "Indeed, only with difficulty does one die for a just person, though perhaps for a good person one might even find courage to die. But God proves his love for us in that while we were still sinners Christ died for us" (Romans 5:7-8).

The joy of the Cross is the joy of a stronger love, it is the joy of the *love which gives (its) life.* The joy of La Salette is not an easy kind of love. It is the joy of converted sinners. It is the joy of those who leave the world of death in which they have been immersed and move towards learning to give (their) life. Passing from sadness to joy is the secret of the Gospel and it is the path Our Lady of La Salette shows us. She invites us to follow her on that path. "I have set before you life and death ... *Choose life, then,* that you and your descendants may live" (Deuteronomy 30:19).

# Epilogue

This book is not a historical study of the La Salette event. Its sole purpose is to break open the theological and spiritual meaning of the message.

In 1956-1957 the late Fr. Charles Rahier, M.S. (the elder, 1898-1969) came to the Major Seminary of the Missionaries of Our Lady of La Salette to give a series of conferences on the Apparition. He observed that, while a good number of historical studies had been undertaken, there was still a considerable amount of work to be done in order to come to a deeper understanding of the meaning of the message. Louis Bassette's book, *Le fait de La Salette (The fact of La Salette)*, had just been published. Since that time, Father Jean

Young Marcel Schlewer amid the Algerian war, speaking to a comrade in arms

Stern, M.S., has completed the publication of all pertinent historical documents in a series of three volumes. Fr. Jean Jaouen's work, *La grace de La Salette au regard de l' Eglise*, **(14)** touched on various areas: history, psychology and spirituality.

I never really appreciated the message of La Salette or grasped its depth until my two years of military service in wartime Algeria. The violence, the routine torture, the summary executions and political blindness made me understand, from within, why Mary weeps and suffers with the human race which refuses to accept Jesus Christ, and why he redeemed us at the price of his blood. Father Voillaume, recalling the violence in Algeria, used to say, "No wonder Our Lady wept at La Salette."

When I returned to the seminary, I was determined to try to understand this message of Mary in the light of Christian revelation. It was at that time that the late Fr. Charles Novel, M.S., mentored me in my internship and training in ministry to the pilgrims at La Salette. He shared with me some of the reflections contained in his doctoral thesis in theology on the theme of redemption.

A little later on I had the good fortune to attend the late Father Bonnard's Scripture course on the prophets at the *Facultes Catholiques (Catholic Schools)* of Lyons. It was under his guidance that I wrote my thesis for my master's degree (in those days it was called a Licentiate) in theology entitled: *Suffering-Punishment for Sin, or God's Way of Teaching us about Salvation?* Since that time, I have continued to study the biblical roots of the message of La Salette. Seen in the light of the Sacred Scriptures and Vatican II, the La Salette message takes on a surprising dimension. I continue to be fed by the amazing spiritual interest it has aroused in thousands of pilgrims from the simplest to the most sophisticated.

A number of other sources have also been useful to me in writing this book, notably:

1. Jean-Paul II: *Christi Fideles laïci* ( 1987) and Redemptoris Missio (1990). Documentation catholique.

2. Joseph Ratzinger: *Foi Chretienne hier et aujourd'hui*, Mame, 1969. *Le Nouveau Peuple de Dieu*, Aubier, 1971.

3. François Varonne: *Ce Dieu absent qui fait probleme*, Cerf, 1981. *Ce Dieu cense aimer La souffrance*, Cerf, 1985.

4. *Pain rompu pour un monde nouveau*. Document theologique de base pour le Congrès Eucharistique International, Centurion, 1989.

5. Dom Lacan: *La Conversion dans la Bible*. Congres de l' AND DP à Poitiers, 1968.

6. Abdon Santaner, O.F.M.: Congres de l' ANDDP: *Pelerinage, Foi et Vie, Toulouse*, octobre 1970.

7. Pasteur Crespy: *Le Loisir dans l'Ecriture sainte.* Congres de la PRTL à Praz-sur-Arly, octobre 1970.

8. Mgr. Feidt, archevêque de Chambery. Son intervention au congrès de la PRTL a Notre-Dame-du-Laus en 1990.

This book is also indebted to the many questions asked by the pilgrims on hearing the message of La Salette, by the young volunteers who help at the Shrine and by my fellow La Salette Missionaries who have taken part in the "La Salette Month"—a continuing education program that each year brings together at La Salette twenty or more Missionaries of Our Lady of La Salette from around the world.

I wish to express my gratitude to all those who assisted me in the writing of this book, especially my confreres and a number of the lay staff at the La Salette Shrine. Particularly warm thanks go to Sister M.D. who spent many long hours revising and rewriting these chapters.

My thanks also go to my religious Congregation which gave me, along with the joy of participating in the ministry of the Shrine on the Holy Mountain for seventeen years, the opportunity to reflect on and deepen my understanding of the message.

Finally, I thank God for the graces he never ceases to pour out on us all through Our Lady of La Salette.

*Fr. Marcel Schlewer, M.S.*

At the Shrine of Our Lady of La Salette, France
August 25, 1995

# Endnotes

1 *"Le Souvenir de la Grande Famine (The Remembrance of the Great Famine)"*, an article which appeared in the daily, La Croix, the issue for September 10-11, 1995. In 1995, the people of Ireland commemorated the 150th anniversary of the great famine and the exodus to the United States.

2 Andre-Jean Tudesq, *La France romantique et bourgeoise 1815-1858*, under the direction of Georges Duby of the French Academy, in *Histoire de la France des origines a nos jours, collection In Extenso*, Larousse, 1995

3 Christian Duquoc, *Dieu different*, Cerf, 1977 (pp.65-66).

4 Jean Stem, La Salette, *Documents Authentiques, fin mars 1847 - avril, 1849*, Cerf, 1984, pp. XIII-XIV.

5 *Rapport Annuel Mondial sur le Systeme Economique et la Strategie (Ramses 82)*.

6 See *La Croix*, April 8, 1995 and July 7, 1995. See also *Croissance*, no. 387, November 1995, which published an independent enquiry into the circumstances of his death; these are still unclear, but it remains true that he had the courage to denounce the exploitation "of six million children who constitute a source of cheap labor."

7 At 1995 exchange rates, 80 francs would be a little under US $17.00 and 20 centimes would be about 95 cents.

8 The author of this book devoted himself to a very enlightening project which he highly recommends to his readers: to look up, with the aid of a concordance, all the biblical passages containing words from the message of La Salette. This gives the message an unforeseen resonance. With this method the author helped La Salette novices acquire a deeper appreciation of the message.

9 Author's note: The examples cited in this chapter will become dated in due time. I have nevertheless included them because the death

of children is still a matter of horrendous urgency.

10 Some Christian churches do not hesitate to ordain as ministers both men and women, whether married or celibate.

11 *Pain Rompu Pour un Monde Nouveau*, pp, 37-38. Key theological document for the International Eucharistic Congress. Centurion, 1989.

12 *Ibidem*, pp. 46-47.

13 *Ibidem*, pp. 65-66

14 Translated into English by Fr. Normand Theroux, M.S. under the title, *A Grace Called La Salette*, La Salette Publications, Attleboro, Massachusetts (1991).

# About the Author

Author Marcel Schlewer has fought numerous battles: for his country as a young soldier in Algeria; for the Palestinians in his zeal for justice; for a more significant role for the laity in the Church, etc. These pages bear the mark of those struggles. At first glance this might appear odd. For what could be more peaceful, more heavenly than an Apparition of the Blessed Virgin Mary—a manifestation of the Mother of God at (of all places!) La Salette, high up in the mountains? It is a spot that seems so removed from our human struggles.

With characteristic intensity, Marcel Schlewer shows us the keen interest Mary takes in our lives and demonstrates how her message is more relevant today than ever. Going on pilgrimage to her Shrine in the French Alps is not going to a place of refuge. Her words offer more than "pious spiritual consolation." Conversion, at La Salette or any other shrine, opens up a new perspective on our human experience and on the realities of our world. It is a perspective enlightened by prayer and the examination of our lives in the light of the Word of God—the Word of God to which Mary keeps alluding.

On that Holy Mountain, Fr. Schlewer accompanied individuals and groups on the path of conversion for over 25 years. Now, in the lowland, as he devotes his energies to the renewal of pastoral ministry, he continues to draw his missionary vitality from Our Lady's message.

May that message lead us, as well, to develop a spiritual life committed to the service of the world and therefore of the Church!

*Father Pierre Kerloc'h, M.S.*
Provincial Superior
Province of Our Lady of La Salette France

# Acknowledgments

Grateful thanks to those good enough to read over my translation and point out the need for correction or clarification: La Salette Fathers René J. Butler, Robert Campbell, Leo Maxfield, Roland S. Nadeau, Donald L. Paradis, Claude F. Rheaume and Normand Theroux.